YOUR COMMONSENSE GUIDE TO PERSONAL FINANCIAL PLANNING

CHARLES ROSS

YOUR COMMONSENSE GUIDE TO PERSONAL FINANCIAL PLANNING

Learn how to budget, protect, and save your money

THOMAS NELSON PUBLISHERS
Nashville

PUBLISHER'S NOTE: This book is intended for general information only. Readers are urged to check the minimal insurance requirements for their state and consult with their personal financial advisors.

Published in Nashville, Tennessee, by Oliver-Nelson Books, a division of Thomas Nelson, Inc., Publishers, and distributed in Canada by Word Communications, Ltd., Richmond, British Columbia.

Library of Congress Cataloging-in-Publication Data

Ross, Charles, 1957–
Your commonsense guide to personal financial planning / Charles Ross.
p. cm.
ISBN 0-8407-9187-9 (paper)
1. Finance, Personal. I. Title.
HG179.R69 1993
332.024—dc20 93–19975
CIP

Printed in the United States of America.

3 4 5 6 — 98 97 96 95

This book is dedicated to my mother,
Newtie Ross,
and to the memory of my father,
Ernest Christopher Ross,
who instilled in me
the seeds of entrepreneurship
and the desire to succeed.

CONTENTS

ACKNOWLEDGMENTS

It is difficult to make sure that everyone who had a hand in making this book a reality gets the proper credit. First, I would like to thank the Lord Jesus Christ, my personal Savior, for the inspiration and strength to complete this book. To my wife, Barbara, I would like to thank her for her devotion and encouragement; she shares the vision of providing financial help and hope to consumers across the country. My thanks go to my daughters, Charlene, Charmaine, and Charnae, who patiently waited as I completed this book when I often had to postpone playtime. To Richard Jordan, who continues to be a trusted friend and business associate, my heartfelt thanks for his thoughtful words of encouragement. Many thanks to Sharon West, producer of our daily and weekly radio programs, for her gentle hand that assures the quality of each show. Special thanks to Larry Calhoun, who reviewed the initial draft and took the words I wrote and made them come alive. To Brian Hampton, my editor at Oliver-Nelson, thanks for the final touch. And finally, to Victor Oliver, my publisher, thank you for seeing the Christ in me and giving me the opportunity to share this book with America.

1

FINANCIAL PLANNING

PERSONAL FINANCIAL PLANNING

Smart use of your money starts with a plan. For the last several decades, the value of the American dollar has been affected by many factors, including inflation, interest rates, and taxes. These factors, which may fluctuate dramatically, have prompted millions of Americans to plan for their future using methods previously employed by the very wealthy.

This method, called personal financial planning, has gained tremendous interest over the past ten years. People no longer put money in passbook savings alone. They invest in certificates of deposit, money market funds, and mutual funds. Terms such as *compound interest, assets* and *liabilities, net worth,* and *rate of return* are fast becoming part of everyday conversation.

What Is Personal Financial Planning?

Personal financial planning is a process that will lead to the development of a strategy for achieving financial success. Success, however, must be defined in your terms according to your goals. This strategy is called a financial plan.

Each person has a fixed idea of financial success. To one, it may be wealth in the extreme: being able to buy whatever is wanted no matter what the cost. To another, it may mean attaining a certain standard of living: having the peace of mind that events such as retirement, the children's education, and even disability or death have been taken care of financially. Understanding your current finances and your future financial needs will put you in a better position to decide how to reach your goals.

Why Is Financial Planning Important?

When you are able to map out your financial future, you can make plans and set goals. In essence, you learn to take control of your life. Should you want to open a business, retire early, or send your children to college, you can plan to do so. In addition, financial planning helps you achieve your goals. In most instances, the difference between achieving or not achieving your goals boils down to a simple question: Will the money be there when you need it?

Finally, financial planning helps you maximize returns on your assets and investments. By looking at asset yields, you can determine if a particular investment should be kept or replaced with a more productive one. Maybe you shouldn't keep so much money in low-interest accounts. Reviewing your financial plan will help you answer this kind of question.

The Plan

Preparing a financial plan involves answering three basic questions:

1. Where are you now financially? You'll need to complete information on your assets and liabilities: how much income you have and what your expenses are. You'll also need a budget to manage your money.
2. Where do you want to be and when do you want to be there? Identifying your goals provides a focus or direction for your plan. Do you want to retire early or in twenty years, buy a house in two years, or send the kids to college in ten years?
3. How do you plan to get there? You must seriously review the investment options available. Which ones can help you reach your goals?

After you implement your plan, making periodic reviews and evaluations is a vital part of the planning process.

Record Keeping and Your Financial Plan

One of the most fundamental steps in the financial planning process is gathering and organizing information. Having documents at your fingertips will prevent you or members of your family from going through dresser drawers and file cabinets to locate a specific item.

Here's a partial list of what to keep handy:

- Bank files, including account statements and canceled checks, should be kept together.
- Employee benefits book and W-2 statements should be easy to find.
- Wills and trust documents should be placed in a central file along with insurance policies.
- Deeds, titles, and mortgage information should be easily accessible.

- Investment records with investment transactions and statements should be clearly marked.

- Copies of tax returns for the last several years along with supporting documents should be easy to find.

Starting and maintaining your financial plan now will make sure your financial future is secure.

THE IMPORTANCE OF SETTING FINANCIAL GOALS

Any serious financial plan must include realistic goals. To save money and invest, you must be motivated. Goals give you focus and direction. Goals are objectives, purposes; they are dreams put into action.

The hardest task for most people to accomplish is prioritizing their goals, determining which are the most important. At the top of the list should be retirement, insurance, and savings goals. Taking the time to prepare realistic goals is vital to your financial plan.

Your goals will have two components: the dollar amount needed, and a time frame for achievement. For example, if you want to buy a house, you'll need to know how much it will cost and when you'll choose to shop for one. Once your goals are in place and you have attached dollar values and time frames, you must look at your current financial position.

How Much Are You Worth?

A financial checkup is part of any financial plan. To know where you're heading, you must know where you are now. The reports that will help you determine this are a balance sheet, an income and expense statement, and a budget. Gathering the information for these reports is the first task. You will need documents such as insurance and investment records and a list of your bank accounts and personal property. Copies of tax returns and employment information will also prove useful. The balance sheet tells you at any given time what you own, what you owe, and what you are worth (see fig. 1.1). An income and expense statement is a record of your income and expenses over a certain time period. A budget is a road map that helps you advance toward your goals (see fig. 1.2). A budget doesn't tell you how to spend your money. You tell your budget how you spend your money.

Armed with this information you can now determine how to achieve your short-term, medium-term, and long-term goals.

Setting Goals

One component of goal setting is establishing a time frame and a dollar amount (see fig. 1.3). Setting time frames for achieving your goals allows you to focus your attention on the one that is most important. In addition, it will give you a sense of urgency that will drive you to accomplish your goals. By attaching a dollar value to a goal, you will know when you have achieved the objective.

Long-term goals may be defined as goals that you want to reach five years or more in the future. Medium-term goals are those that you desire to achieve within one to four years. Short-term goals are those that you seek to accomplish within the next year.

Most people set long-term goals first and then short-term and medium-term goals. For example, suppose you want to retire from your current job in fifteen years with $100,000 in

Figure 1.1

PERSONAL BALANCE SHEET

Assets		**Liabilities**	
Cash on hand	________	Current debts	________
Checking accounts	________	Credit cards	________
Savings accounts	________	Auto loans	________
Loans receivable	________	Mortgages	
Cash value life insurance	________	Investment real estate	________
Investment real estate	________	Personal residence	________
Personal residence	________	Home equity	________
Investments (market value)		Other bank loans	________
Stocks	________	Other liabilities	________
Bonds	________		________
Mutual funds	________		________
Certificates of deposit	________		________
			________
Retirement plan (vested interest)	________		________
IRAs	________		________
Other	________		________
Personal property (present value)		**TOTAL LIABILITIES**	________
Home furnishings	________		
Appliances	________		
Clothing	________		
Jewelry	________		
Automobiles	________		
Other	________		
TOTAL ASSETS	________	**NET WORTH** (assets minus liabilities)	________

Figure 1.2

MONTHLY BUDGET OF INCOME AND EXPENSES

	Budget	Actual	Difference
INCOME			
Salary			
Spouse			
Other			
TOTAL INCOME			
Less:			
Taxes			
Federal			
State			
City			
FICA			
Other			
TOTAL TAXES			
NET INCOME			
EXPENSES			
Housing			
Mortgage (rent)			
Insurance			
Taxes			
Electricity			
Gas			
Water			
Sanitation			
Telephone			
Maintenance			
Other			
TOTAL			
Food			
Automobiles			
Car payments			
Gasoline and oil			
Insurance			

	Budget	Actual	Difference
Licenses			
Taxes			
Maint./repair			
TOTAL			
Insurance			
Life			
Health			
Other			
TOTAL			
Debts			
Credit cards			
Bank loans			
Other			
TOTAL			
Entertainment/ recreation			
Restaurants			
Travel			
Baby-sitters			
Vacation			
Activities			
Other			
TOTAL			
Clothing			
Savings			
Medical expenses			
Doctor			
Dentist			
Drugs			
Other			
TOTAL			
Miscellaneous			
Charitable giving			

	Budget	Actual	Difference
Beauty, barber			
Laundry, cleaning			
Allowances			
Subscriptions			
Gifts			
Education			
Other			
TOTAL			
TOTAL EXPENSES			

INCOME VS. EXPENSES

NET INCOME			
LESS EXPENSES			
NET PROFIT (LOSS)			

cash savings. A short-term goal may be to save at least $5,000 by the end of the first year. A medium-term goal may be to save $28,000 in four years and $65,000 in ten.

The Most Important Goals

As you decide on the goals you will include in your financial plan, you should give three goals priority. Make sure you have

- adequate insurance coverage.
- a plan for retirement.
- a regular savings program.

To protect your property and your family, you need the proper amount of life, disability, health, and liability insurance (see the specific sections on these subjects for more details). Determine how much you need, and buy all you need.

You need to develop a retirement program. Find out from your employer and the government what benefits you will be

FIGURE 1.3

GOALS AND OBJECTIVES

SHORT-TERM (within one year)

GOAL: ______________________________

Objective	Time Frame	Dollar Amount	Weekly Amount
____________	________	$________	$________
____________	________	$________	$________
____________	________	$________	$________
____________	________	$________	$________
____________	________	$________	$________

MEDIUM-TERM (one to four years)

GOAL: ______________________________

Objective	Time Frame	Dollar Amount	Weekly Amount
____________	________	$________	$________
____________	________	$________	$________
____________	________	$________	$________
____________	________	$________	$________
____________	________	$________	$________

LONG-TERM (five years or more)

GOAL: ______________________________

Objective	Time Frame	Dollar Amount	Weekly Amount
____________	________	$________	$________
____________	________	$________	$________
____________	________	$________	$________
____________	________	$________	$________
____________	________	$________	$________

entitled to when you retire. In addition, look into programs such as individual retirement accounts (IRAs) and 401(k)s to discover other ways you can set aside money for retirement.

Finally, start a regular savings program. There are many ways to become financially secure, but ignoring a savings program is not one of them. A good rule of thumb is to save at least 10 percent of your monthly gross income. Whatever amount you decide to save, do it on a regular basis.

Implementing the Plan

Success in reaching your goals means activating your plan. No goal-setting process is complete unless the goals are put into action. Often, the path to financial freedom is littered with would-be millionaires whose only drawback was not the lack of a plan but the inability to implement one.

Get a clear fix on what you want to accomplish. Visualize yourself achieving your goal. Imagine what your life-style will be, what type of house you'll live in, the income and financial security you'll have. What do you want your money to do for you? Remember to set a realistic time frame for reaching each goal.

A plan is as essential to success as air is to life. Without a plan, you just wander through life. Get a clear idea of what you want to do, then do it now! Not tomorrow, next week, or next year. Do it now! With a realistic plan and some self-discipline, you can attain your dream.

BUDGETING YOUR WAY TO FINANCIAL INDEPENDENCE

If you are not financially secure and want to be, you will have to accomplish this goal for yourself. Consider this: behind every family fortune was one ancestor who had little money but knew the value of budgeting. That person set aside an amount from earnings and put it into something he or she thought would increase in value and was successful.

I have a friend who works in the trust department of a major bank. He says that becoming financially secure involves sacrifice: spending less than you earn and investing the rest. To get on a wealth-building plan, start keeping records so you know how much money comes in and how much goes out. You can take shortcuts to financial security, but ignoring a budget program is not one of them. You work hard for your money, so why not spend some time managing it? Many of us spend more time washing our cars than we do managing our money.

Why Budget?

Many people assume that you have to earn a lot of money to budget. But if you wait until you have enough money to budget, you probably never will. Since most people tend to spend as much as they earn, budgeting takes on more significance. People are discovering they have to control their erratic spending habits.

Some people try to keep a budget in their heads. "Was it $60 or $70 I planned to spend on clothes this month?" The only way to really maintain a budget is to write it down.

The Ford Foundation recently completed a study on achievement. The study reported that 10 percent of the population had specific well-defined goals; 7 percent reached their goals 50 percent of the time; 3 percent reached their goals 90 percent of the time. What made the difference with the latter group? They wrote their goals down. That is the *only* difference between those who don't achieve their goals and those who achieve their goals 90 percent of the time. They write their goals down. A goal becomes important to you once you see it on paper. It takes on a life of its own.

Look at your household like a business. A business could not survive if the owner didn't plan how to spend its income. You have income and expenses just like a business does. As long as your income exceeds your expenses, you remain in good financial shape.

The major benefit derived from developing and following a budget is the peace of mind that comes when you know that you have a firm grasp on your financial situation and you know where you spend your hard-earned dollars. Having control over your finances will give you confidence in your future.

Setting Up a Budget

Before you embark on a budgeting program, you want to determine your goals, whether they include increased savings, reduction of debt, or just better money management (see "Setting Goals").

Next, you want to find out your monthly net income or take-home pay (see fig. 1.2). This is the amount of money you actually receive from your employer after all taxes and deductions are taken out.

Adding up your total monthly expenses is the next step. Gather up your receipts, look through your canceled checks, and try to see exactly where your money went last month. Write these figures down and separate them into categories: housing, food, automobiles, and so on.

Now, subtract your monthly expenses from your net income. Do you have anything left? Good! If not, you are spending more than you earn. You need to cut expenses or find ways to increase your income if you're going to stay in good financial health.

Implementing Your Budget

Many people cash their paychecks, put a little in the checking account, and pocket the rest. Try depositing all of your income into your checking account and paying your bills and expenses by check. This method will allow you to keep track of your income and expenses and will also make it easier later when you have to review your budget and make adjustments.

Another idea is to use an expense diary. An expense diary, which you can get from any office supply store, helps you track expenses, small and large, on a daily basis. A pocket-size diary is easy to carry, and you can record expenses and store receipts in it. Maintaining your checkbook will support your expense diary records. Noting your expenses will be important for completing your budget and doing your taxes at tax time.

Impulse buying can ruin the best budget plan. By depositing all your income in a checking account, you keep the money out of your hands so you can't spend it. If you are already using this system, good for you. If not, why not give it a trial run?

Reviewing and Evaluating Your Budget

Developing a budget and maintaining it aren't always easy. Budgets, like cars, require regular maintenance. For your budget to run smoothly, you have to take the time to review and evaluate. Unexpected expenses or sudden spending urges can reduce a perfectly sensible, useful budget to shambles.

Set aside some time each month to review your budget, maybe at the same time you balance your checking account. Are you spending too much on entertainment? Maybe you need to save more. Except for your tithing and savings pledges, consider your budget flexible enough to adjust to changing times.

Now that your finances are laid out, you may have to decide what to curtail or give up to reach your goals. Don't make it too painful. But if it doesn't hurt a little, you are probably not trying hard enough. Learn to live within your budget.

COMMON MISTAKES IN FINANCIAL PLANNING

When it comes to money management, avoiding major mistakes is just as essential as making the right moves. People make some common errors. Watch out for the following ones.

Limited Family Involvement

Having only one family member involved in financial matters is courting disaster. Even though one spouse may be responsible for decision making, both spouses should meet with their accountants, bankers, insurance agents, stockbrokers, and lawyers.

No Written Goals

When you consider your financial goals, you need to place a dollar amount and a time frame on each objective. For example, if you plan to buy a house, you need to know how much you will need for a down payment and when you plan to buy. In addition, once you have financial goals on paper, you must weigh their relative importance.

No Budget

Not having a budget is a serious mistake. It is very difficult to become financially secure without knowing how much you earn and spend. To get a better grip on your money, be sure to have a written budget. If you don't have it in writing, you can easily forget whether you planned on spending $100 or $150 on food this month. Budgets work!

No Money for Emergencies

You should have a savings fund equal to six months of expenses. That way, if you become unemployed, get sick, or need extra cash, you will not have to borrow. To get your savings fund started, decide how much you can afford and start saving right now, no matter how small the amount may be.

No Tax Planning

It is wise to have a plan to reduce your taxes. A sound strategy is to do what CPAs call tax planning. Find ways to structure your affairs so as to minimize the taxes paid. As a matter of fact, now is a good time to consult with your tax preparer concerning this year's taxes.

Every year after you have completed your tax return, consult with your tax preparer to develop ways to reduce your taxes for the next year. It might mean converting your hobby to a business in order to take advantage of business deductions, or it might involve contributing to the company's profit-sharing plan. Becoming financially secure without a knowledge of the tax laws is very difficult.

Not Utilizing Employee Benefits

As a wise money manager, you should be aware of all your benefits. Many employees, for instance, don't know if they have group life insurance or how much coverage they have.

Many don't compare coverage that might be duplicated, such as with health insurance. One spouse may have a better health insurance plan than the other, but because they have always used one particular plan, they have never bothered to compare to determine if they can lower their health insurance premiums.

Another area that employees neglect is profit-sharing plans like 401(k)s. These plans allow you to save for retirement and reduce your taxes. The human resources department at your company may be able to help you decide which plan is right for you.

Not Spreading the Risk

Often people invest too much money in one area. A common practice is to obtain a lot of shares of company stock. That is not a bad strategy, but having all your investment money in one stock can be risky. If you don't have money in a money market account, certificates of deposit, mutual funds, or real estate, now is the time to give your investments a fresh look.

Many investors try to decide where the market is going and then invest in vehicles that would benefit from that scenario. But today, people are having trouble predicting in what direction the economy is going. So it pays to spread your money around.

MANAGING THE FAMILY'S FINANCES

One of the most constant challenges a family will face is managing its money. Many family arguments can be traced back to money. But what seem to be money problems often have little to do with money and more to do with how people feel. Even among the wealthy, the money fights bear a great deal of resemblance to the fights of the not-so-wealthy. The fights may be more sophisticated and involve luxuries instead of necessities, but the conflicts are basically the same.

Working As a Team

Making money together is more challenging and can be more difficult than making money separately. Separate financial goals of a husband and a wife can break up a marriage. Making money is a business.

The basic attitudes needed to build a successful money team are trust, autonomy, fair dealing, and a sense of prosperity. Suspicion regarding any major money-related issue can cause serious problems in a relationship and interfere with the smooth conduct of business. If the husband suspects the wife is overspending, he may hide his true income. The wife, in turn, may feel betrayed and skim from her budget, hiding money away for her use.

Developing Trust

Trust is emotionally liberating. A good deal of relief comes with not having to look over someone's shoulder. Most couples who plan to stay together trust each other. If trust isn't a part of your relationship, your first goal should be to develop this aspect of your marriage.

Having Money of Your Own

A key to successful family money management is that teammates feel they have money of their own. It's important that a couple has one joint checking account where paychecks are deposited and from which the bills are paid. But it's equally important that each person has money to call his or her own.

Having money of your own can be accomplished through setting aside an allowance. Each partner should be able to spend a specific amount of money without having to account for it. The key here is that each partner must agree on the amount of the allowance. Making the allowance the same amount for each partner is a workable solution.

Treating Each Other Fairly

So, where there are trust and autonomy, a sense of fair dealing will follow. Both parties will share equally in the relationship and in the benefits of good money management. When things go well, both partners can expect to have their financial needs met. For example, if one spouse gets a bonus, it can be shared.

The significant part of achieving a sense of fairness is prioritizing the financial goals and aspirations so that they are acceptable to both partners. Often the negotiations that accompany goal setting and budgeting bring into the relationship a fairness that will become habitual.

Dealing with Prosperity

The word *prosperity,* when applied to successful family money management, means something other than "rich," "wealthy," or "comfortable." Prosperity is dynamic, having more to do with change. A successful money management team that is prosperous will be doing better over a period of time.

A couple can feel prosperous at any economic level, whether rich or poor. It just takes hope, a belief in the future, and some financial results. Successful couples have a sense of prosperity and are willing to do what it takes to bring them closer to wealth. Nothing helps to enhance the feeling of prosperity more than actually making money. The first step toward prosperity is developing a practical budget.

FINANCIAL LIFE CYCLES

Your family situation affects the financial choices you make. Your financial needs change throughout your life. As an unmarried person, you develop patterns of budgeting and investing that may last a lifetime. Here are some helpful planning tips for singles.

First, start a budget and stick to it. Next, put a portion of your monthly income into a savings account. Consider this money an emergency reserve fund that can pay your monthly bills for at least three, and possibly six, months.

As a single person, you'll want to have adequate insurance coverage in two forms—health and disability. Your employer may provide this coverage for you. It is also a good idea to have sufficient life insurance.

Young Married Couple's Life Cycle

The challenge facing a married couple is combining spending patterns and incomes. As a young married couple, you and your spouse belong to a group with certain characteristics. Much like single people, you and your spouse tend to think on a short-term basis. As a two-income family, you have a high degree of buying and saving power. Financially, you will want to start planning for retirement by making contributions to an IRA. Seek a qualified professional to help you with tax planning.

If you haven't started a budget, you need to do so. During this period of your life, you should start thinking about buying a home. It is also a good time to review your insurance coverage to make sure your life, health, and disability plans are adequate. In addition, draw up a will to make sure your spouse and loved ones are provided for in case of premature death.

The Childbearing Life Cycle

Raising children is a great financial responsibility, but a well-thought-out plan can help. Having children will change your life forever. During this life cycle, when you are adding to your family, your financial objectives will change even more drastically than they did when you were first married.

For the first time in your life, you will have to think about the distant future. Your family budget will need to be updated to reflect higher monthly expenses. Here are a few planning ideas for this time in your life.

Start saving for your children's college education now. The earlier you begin this plan, the lesser will be the strain on your monthly budget later.

Increase your life insurance and health insurance coverage. Update your will. Even though your budget may be tight, keep up the payments to your IRA. Even a reduced contribution each month will show tremendous growth by the time you retire.

Mid-Career Life Cycle

As you move into the mid-career life cycle, your characteristics may change again. You have married, started a family, and purchased a home. Your children are near college age, your pension and IRA accounts are building in value, and your equity in your home is rising.

At this time, put as much as you can afford into savings and investments, enhancing the safety with a decent rate of return. Avoid second mortgages or refinancing. If you haven't planned for your children's college education, do so now.

Among the financial threats you could face during this cycle are poor business decisions if you are self-employed and layoffs if you are an employee. Of course, poor investment decisions could severely affect your finances at this point in your life. Putting money aside for contingencies will limit the impact of the unexpected.

LIFE INSURANCE

The basic role of life insurance at one time was to provide for your dependents in the event of your untimely death. But today, life insurance is being used as a fund for retirement or children's college educational needs, as an investment vehicle, or as a money source for a variety of other purposes.

Yet buying life insurance can be like walking through a mine field. One false step and you can end up a loser.

You can take two steps that will put you on the road to making the best decision possible in the purchase of life insurance. First, you need to understand the basics of life insurance, and second, you need to find a professional agent to help you select the right policy.

Term Life Insurance

Term or temporary insurance was designed to provide policy owners with short-term rather than lifelong protection. It is generally used when a young family needs a large amount of life insurance coverage but is not able to afford a cash-value policy. When you purchase term insurance, you are buying it for a certain period of time, one to twenty years. At the end of the term, the policy can be renewed or allowed to expire. The premiums increase with each renewal because you are getting older.

Term insurance does not build up a cash value and is generally not available after age sixty-five. Properly used, term insurance fills a need for low-cost, short-term protection.

Purchasing term insurance to cover your entire lifetime can well be the most expensive type of policy.

Whole Life Insurance

There are many variations of cash-value life insurance policies. Most provide the same death benefit throughout your life for a set premium payment.

In a cash-value life insurance policy, you will pay the same premium at age sixty-five as you did when you were thirty. The simplest form of cash-value life insurance is whole life, or permanent life, insurance.

The policy remains in force throughout your lifetime. It has the advantage of building up a cash value, which you can use later in a number of ways. When you retire, for example, you can surrender the policy and take the accumulated cash value.

Universal Life Insurance

With this type of policy, you have a hybrid product. It is a cross between the lower rates of term insurance and the cash buildup of a whole life policy. You decide how much you want to pay into your policy each year, with certain minimums applying. You can add extra money one month, then skip several months altogether. If you don't pay enough to cover the cost of the coverage, the extra sum will be subtracted from your cash value.

Shopping for Life Insurance Can Save You Money

When shopping for life insurance, don't combine insurance with investments. Buy a life insurance policy for the coverage it provides and not for the investment returns. Buy life insurance to provide for your loved ones in the case of your death, and purchase investments to satisfy investment goals and objectives. To purchase the best policy, first determine how much insurance you need (see fig. 1.4).

It is always wise to inquire about the actual cost of your insurance. A professional agent should be prepared to give you this information.

Cost information will be given in the form of an index, either a surrender cost or a net payment cost index. The *net payment cost index* is based on the amount paid at your death, and it is useful in comparing policies.

The *surrender cost index* is based on what you would get if you turned in the policy. This index is used to compare cash values between policies. With both indexes, a policy with a smaller number is generally the better buy than a comparable policy with a larger number.

Knowing how to compare policies and how much to pay will result in your gaining more coverage for less money.

Selecting the Right Policy

When the time comes to actually buy life insurance, look for and select a good agent. Here are some guidelines. First, use an agent who is committed to a career in life insurance sales and is not just a part-time agent. Seek an agent with at least five years' experience in life insurance sales.

Second, look for someone who is a Chartered Life Underwriter (CLU) or is working toward becoming one. This designation identifies a person with substantial knowledge in the field of insurance and other related financial areas.

Third, select an agent who is active in the Million Dollar Round Table. That means you are dealing with an agent with a successful track record.

In determining how much you should pay for life insur-

Figure 1.4

QUICK LIFE INSURANCE PLANNER

		Sample
1. Family's yearly expenses (including yearly amounts set aside for retirement and college funds)	______ Line 1	$ 50,000
2. Family's yearly income from		
Social Security	______	______
Surviving spouse's job	______	$ 30,000
Other income	______	______
Total	______ Line 2	$ 30,000
3. Family's investment income		
3a. Total amount of savings/investments	______	$ 5,000
3b. Interest rate that capital would earn (e.g., 6%, 8%) expressed as a decimal (i.e., 6% = .06, 8% = .08)	______	.06
Result: family's income from savings and investments (multiply Line 3a by Line 3b)	______ Line 3	$ 300
4. Shortfall from budget (subtract Lines 2 and 3 from Line 1)	______ Line 4	$ 19,700
5. Divide Line 4 by 12	______ Line 5	$ 1,642
6. Divide 12 by Line 3b (for example, 12 divided by .08)	______ Line 6	200
7. Total life insurance needed (multiply Line 6 by Line 5)	______ Line 7	$328,400

ance, see figure 1.5, which illustrates how much you should pay for term insurance. Then review figure 1.6, which compares yearly premiums for a $100,000 policy for a nonsmoking male.

Figure 1.5

THE MOST YOU SHOULD PAY FOR TERM INSURANCE

NONSMOKERS			SMOKERS		
	Annual Premium*			Annual Premium*	
Age	Male	Female	Age	Male	Female
18–30	$ .76	$ .68	18–30	$ 1.05	$ 1.01
31	.76	.69	31	1.10	1.05
32	.77	.70	32	1.15	1.10
33	.78	.71	33	1.21	1.15
34	.79	.72	34	1.28	1.20
35	.80	.74	35	1.35	1.25
36	.84	.78	36	1.45	1.31
37	.88	.82	37	1.56	1.38
38	.92	.86	38	1.68	1.45
39	.97	.90	39	1.81	1.52
40	1.03	.95	40	1.95	1.60
41	1.09	1.00	41	2.12	1.73
42	1.17	1.05	42	2.30	1.89
43	1.25	1.10	43	2.50	2.05
44	1.34	1.15	44	2.72	2.22
45	1.45	1.20	45	2.95	2.40
46	1.59	1.29	46	3.22	2.59
47	1.74	1.41	47	3.52	2.79
48	1.91	1.53	48	3.85	3.01
49	2.10	1.66	49	4.21	3.23
50	2.30	1.76	50	4.60	3.50
51	2.49	1.90	51	4.97	3.79
52	2.70	2.06	52	5.38	4.10
53	2.96	2.22	53	5.82	4.44
54	3.40	2.40	54	6.29	4.80
55	3.40	2.60	55	6.80	5.20
56	3.66	2.79	56	7.31	5.58
57	3.94	3.00	57	7.87	5.99
58	4.23	3.22	58	8.46	6.43
59	4.55	3.46	59	9.10	6.90
60	4.90	3.70	60	9.80	7.40
61	5.43	3.98	61	10.83	7.95
62	6.02	4.28	62	11.98	8.54
63	6.67	4.60	63	13.25	9.18
64	7.40	4.93	64	14.65	9.86
65	8.20	5.30	65	16.20	10.60

*Per $1,000 of coverage, per year
Source: National Insurance Consumer Organization

FIGURE 1.6

YEARLY PREMIUMS FOR A $100,000 POLICY

Age	Term Insurance	Universal Life Insurance	Whole Life Insurance
30	$136	$ 590	$ 875
35	140	746	1,095
40	163	950	1,391
45	205	1,217	1,776
50	320	1,583	2,311
55	440	2,078	3,038
60	610	2,741	4,717
65	980	3,665	5,376

Source: National Insurance Consumer Organization

Also, before choosing a life insurance company, consult *Best's Guide to Life Insurance Companies*. It is available at your library and rates insurance companies on their overall performance.

HEALTH INSURANCE

Your health insurance can help keep your finances fit. With the high cost of medical care today, you have to worry about what will happen to your personal finances if you or a family member becomes sick. If you have health insurance, you can be certain that most of the expenses will be paid.

Notes: Figure 1.5 shows the premium rate per $1,000 of coverage. If you're buying a $100,000 policy, multiply the cost by 100 and add $60 (for the insurer's fixed policy expenses) to see the most that you should pay.

Policies smaller than $100,000 cost a little more. Policies written for $500,000 and up cost a little less.

Nonsmokers' rates are for preferred health risks.

The relative rates for smokers keep rising because insurers see how fast the smokers are dying.

Rates and companies may have changed by the time you read this. For an update, check the latest NICO guide: *Taking the Bite Out of Insurance.*

Here are some features of a health insurance plan. A *basic health plan* is defined as "a policy that includes hospital, surgical, and physicians' expense coverage." Most policies also cover major medical costs. This coverage picks up where your basic coverage ends. Most health insurance policies also have a deductible, requiring you to pay the first $200 to $500 of medical expenses each year. In addition, a coinsurance clause will have you pay a percentage of certain types of charges, such as prescriptions and doctor visits.

Asset or Liability?

If you're covered by a health insurance plan, chances are, your policy includes hospital expense insurance. These benefits go to pay for your hospital stay. Your policy should cover room and board, nursing care, drugs, lab fees, X rays, and medical supplies. Traditional health insurance plans limit hospital expense coverage to a specified period of time, in most cases from 20 to 120 days. Newer plans now limit the total dollar amount they'll cover.

Another feature of health insurance plans is surgical expense insurance. It covers the cost of operations. But beware of the fact that some policies don't cover all procedures. These policies will generally list what types of operations they cover and how much they will pay. They typically cover the usual, customary, and "reasonable" fees for surgical procedures.

Major Medical

Your major medical insurance is a key part of your health insurance coverage. Without this coverage, you can be left footing the entire bill for an extended hospital stay or other medical costs. Major medical insurance picks up where basic coverage—hospital, surgical, and physicians' expenses—ends.

Benefits go to pay for care provided both in and out of the hospital. For example, if your health insurance limits coverage in a hospital to only twenty-one days and you've been in the hospital twenty-five days, the major medical plan takes effect and pays for the extra four days in the hospital. Most major medical plans pay 80 to 100 percent of your medical expense over a deductible amount.

HMOs

Health maintenance organizations, HMOs for short, are prepaid health care plans that provide all your medical care. The organization either employs or contracts with physicians in every specialty, from internal medicine to psychiatry.

Most HMOs require you to use their doctors and services, except in emergencies. HMOs give you the cost advantage of no deductibles and no coinsurance. With most plans you pay a nominal fee, say $3 or so, per visit and per prescription. Paying a nominal fee is a major advantage for those who can't afford to pay medical expenses out of pocket. But before you sign with an HMO, check the reputation of the doctors it employs in addition to asking these questions: Will the HMO cover accidents when I'm out of town? What happens if I need a specialist not retained by the HMO? Answers to these questions will help you avoid financial surprises later.

Do You Have All You Need?

Finding out how much health insurance you need will help you in purchasing the most coverage for the least amount of money. You want to know three things.

First, how much is your deductible? Is it an amount you can afford?

Second, does your policy include a coinsurance plan that requires you to pay 20 percent of the bills? At what point would paying 20 percent of your medical costs put you in serious financial trouble?

And third, make sure your policy has stop-loss provisions (that is, your maximum out-of-pocket medical expense is limited). If this limit is $2,000, for example, you are protected from paying 20 percent of what could be an enormous medical bill. Also, be sure the policy has a $1 million or higher ceiling on benefits paid by the plan over your lifetime.

LIVING WELL ON LESS

With advance planning and the right investment moves, you can take a cut in income, change careers, or stay home with the baby and still make ends meet.

First, get a grip on your budget. And above all, avoid buying on credit. You may have to postpone vacations for a while or take less-expensive ones.

To develop a clear picture of your income and expenses, you must decide which expenses are essential and which ones can be cut. You may be able to make significant budget cuts by postponing home improvements, moving to a less-expensive neighborhood, or refinancing your mortgage.

Supplementing Your Income

Starting to plan several years ahead for this kind of change in life-style is ideal. If you don't have the luxury of a long lead time before your income drops, here are some options to consider.

Think about making an early withdrawal from your individual retirement account or drawing on your savings. There are times when using these funds is a good idea. A career change is one of these times.

If you're young, you can rebuild your savings later. If you

view the drop in income as permanent, consider drawing down your capital the price you pay to gain a more fulfilling job or a more satisfying life.

Investment Options

Before leaving your job, you would be wise to consider making changes in your investments. For example, you may want to start shifting your investments from low-dividend, high-growth securities to a portfolio that features high income.

If you are not inclined to take risks, invest in short-term certificates of deposit and treasury securities. Remember, investments with potential for fluctuations in principal are not worth the risk if you need the money in a year or less.

When starting your own business, limit outside investments to a money market account. Beyond that, direct most of your assets to the new business. Your profit potential is far greater when you own a business.

Losing Fringe Benefits

Fringe benefits that accompany your present job can be worth hundreds of dollars each month. Leaving one employer for another may enable you to pick up a comparable benefits package. But becoming self-employed or leaving the work force altogether may present a problem if you have to pick up the tab for these benefits.

First, look at your pension benefits. If you are entitled to a lump-sum pension distribution when you leave your job, you can roll it over to an individual retirement account (IRA) within sixty days. If you don't roll it over, you will pay tax on it as well as a 10 percent penalty if you're under 59½ years of age. If you will no longer be covered by a pension plan, you will have to provide one for yourself. An IRA is one alternative.

Replacing Your Health Insurance Coverage

Signing up for benefits under your spouse's plan is the best way to replace your health insurance after leaving your job. If you are forced to buy coverage on the open market, you are in for a shock. Without the benefit of group rates, a family plan could cost as much as $200 to $300 a month.

You can get temporary relief under a new federal law called the Consolidated Omnibus Budget Reconciliation Act of 1985 (COBRA). This act requires most employers to let you continue getting group benefits when you leave your job, provided you pick up the premiums plus a 2 percent administration fee.

It's a good idea to buy disability insurance before you leave your job because you may have trouble qualifying later. Update your life insurance coverage, too.

Whatever your reasons for deciding to live on less, the longer the lead time before you make the switch, the better off you will be.

RETIREMENT

Retirement can be a time of uncertainty. The average couple retires with the home paid for but very little in the bank. A financial plan can ease the stress.

Your retirement years are a period of major adjustment, both personally and financially. From this point on, you will be living on a fixed income. Even though you may have planned during your working years, you will find that inflation requires the use of more income than expected to meet your expenses.

To protect yourself, think about these ideas:

- Consider a part-time job if supplementing your income becomes a necessity.
- Avoid unnecessary spending by budgeting to live on your income.
- Review your insurance again, especially your health coverage. Make sure it is adequate.
- Try to eliminate all debt. A retirement budget should be free from all interest expense and other unnecessary monthly payments.

Retirement Planning

Too many investors approach their retirement program as if it were totally separate from their general investment strategy. Nothing could be further from the truth. (For a quick retirement planner, see fig. 1.7.)

Your retirement program should be totally compatible with your investment goals. Retirement planning is simply a long-term investment strategy. Your other goals may vary in term from long to short, depending on your objectives.

One of the first things you want to do when estimating how much you will need for retirement is to make sure you will be able to maintain your present standard of living. To retire financially independent, you will need 65 percent of your present income. Why? Because by the time you retire, your mortgage will be paid for, your kids will have finished college, and you probably will not have any long-term debt. Therefore, you will be able to live a simpler life.

Next, several factors will affect how much you will be able to accumulate for retirement. They are *inflation, annual contribution* (how much you can afford to stash away for retirement), *time* (how many years before retirement), and *yield* (what return your money will earn).

Figure 1.7

QUICK RETIREMENT PLANNER

		Sample
Annual income	______ Line 1	$ 30,000
Years to retirement	______ Line 2	30
Inflation rate	______ Line 3	6%
Amount needed to maintain current standard of living (multiply Line 1 by .65)	______ Line 4	$ 19,500
Current annual income adjusted for inflation (multiply Line 4 by inflation multiplier; see fig. 1.8 and use inflation rate from Line 3)	______ Line 5	$ 111,988
Projected rate of return at retirement (what you anticipate at retirement your lump sum will earn; expressed as decimal—i.e., 8% = .08, 10% = .10)	______ Line 6	.10
Total lump-sum retirement needed (divide Line 5 by Line 6)	______ Line 7	$1,119,885

FIGURE 1.8

ADJUSTING TODAY'S ESTIMATED RETIREMENT NEEDS FOR TOMORROW'S INFLATION

Years	Assumed Rates of Inflation								
to Go	6%	7%	8%	9%	10%	12%	14%	15%	16%
1	1.060	1.070	1.080	1.090	1.100	1.120	1.140	1.150	1.160
2	1.124	1.145	1.166	1.186	1.210	1.254	1.300	1.322	1.346
3	1.191	1.225	1.260	1.295	1.331	1.405	1.482	1.521	1.561
4	1.262	1.311	1.360	1.412	1.464	1.574	1.689	1.749	1.811
5	1.338	1.403	1.469	1.539	1.611	1.762	1.925	2.011	2.100
6	1.419	1.501	1.587	1.677	1.772	1.974	2.195	2.313	2.436
7	1.504	1.606	1.714	1.828	1.949	2.211	2.502	2.660	2.826
8	1.594	1.718	1.851	1.993	2.144	2.476	2.853	3.059	3.278
9	1.689	1.838	1.999	2.172	2.358	2.773	3.252	3.518	3.803
10	1.791	1.967	2.159	2.367	2.594	3.106	3.707	4.046	4.411
11	1.898	2.105	2.332	2.580	2.853	3.479	4.226	4.652	5.117
12	2.012	2.252	2.518	2.813	3.138	3.893	4.818	5.380	5.926
13	2.133	2.410	2.720	3.066	3.452	4.363	5.092	6.153	6.886
14	2.261	2.579	2.937	3.342	3.797	4.887	6.261	7.076	7.995
15	2.397	2.759	3.172	3.642	4.177	5.474	7.138	8.137	9.266
16	2.540	2.952	3.426	3.970	4.595	6.130	8.137	9.358	10.748
17	2.693	3.159	3.700	4.328	5.054	6.866	9.276	10.761	12.468
18	2.854	3.380	3.996	4.717	5.560	7.690	10.575	12.375	14.463
19	3.026	3.617	4.316	5.142	6.116	8.613	12.056	14.232	16.777
20	3.207	3.870	4.661	5.604	6.728	9.646	13.743	16.367	19.461
25	4.292	5.427	6.848	8.623	10.835	17.000	26.462	32.919	40.874
30	5.743	7.612	10.063	13.268	17.449	29.960	50.950	66.212	85.850

Let's use an example:

Annual income = $30,000
Years to retirement = 30 (current age = 35)
Inflation rate = 6%

As mentioned before, you will need approximately 65 percent of your current income. So, first we multiply $30,000 by .65:

$$
\begin{array}{r}
\$30{,}000 \\
\underline{\times\ .65} \\
\$19{,}500
\end{array}
$$

Next, we need to determine how much $19,500 is equivalent to in thirty years, adjusted for inflation. To do this, we use the chart in figure 1.8 to find your inflation multiplier. Look down the "Years to Go" column and find your years to go until retirement. Then look across to the column for the inflation rate you wish to assume. Let's assume a 6 percent inflation rate. You now have your inflation multiplier: 5.743.

$$
\begin{array}{r}
\$19{,}500 \\
\underline{\times\ 5.743} \\
\$111{,}988.50
\end{array}
$$

(We'll round it off to $112,000.)

What this says is that if you now make $30,000 a year, to retire in thirty years you will need $112,000 in annual income just to maintain your current standard of living.

The retirement planning challenge is to have a lump-sum amount of money at retirement that, when invested, would generate $112,000 in income a year.

Let's project a rate of return at retirement of 10 percent. You would need to accumulate a lump sum by age sixty-five that would produce $112,000 in income a year at 10 percent interest. To determine the lump sum needed, we simply divide the annual income required by the projected rate of return (expressed as a decimal).

$$
\begin{array}{r}
\$112{,}000 \\
\underline{\div\ .10} \\
\$1{,}120{,}000
\end{array}
$$

So the lump sum needed at retirement is $1,120,000.

The retirement planning challenge means that you must match what you know you will need at retirement and how much you must set aside now to accomplish that (see fig. 1.9). Obviously, the higher the rate of return, the more you will have at retirement. To get better returns, you will have to invest in more aggressive investments other than savings accounts and government securities. (For an overview of some of your investment alternatives, see chapter 2, "Investing.")

FIGURE 1.9

HOW RETIREMENT PLAN ACCUMULATIONS WORK OUT

Age	Total Deposit at Age 65 (at $2,000/Yr.)	Rate of Return 8%	10%	12%
30	$70,000	$413,126	$700,122	$1,216,042
35	$60,000	$266,846	$413,487	$ 653,950
40	$50,000	$169,331	$240,826	$ 347,996
45	$40,000	$104,323	$136,819	$ 181,462
50	$30,000	$ 60,987	$ 74,167	$ 90,815
55	$20,000	$ 32,097	$ 36,428	$ 41,475
60	$10,000	$ 12,839	$ 13,694	$ 14,618

Double the dollar figures for a married couple (if both work) who contribute $4,000 annually.

You need to be concerned about two general classes of retirement programs. The first is a pension plan provided by a corporation, union, or other institution. The second is an individual program, such as an IRA, a Keogh plan, or a Simplified Employee Pension plan.

Defined Contribution Plans

Defined contribution plans are structured so that the employer pays a specific amount into the pension fund for each participant. These payments accumulate, along with investment and interest earnings, in separate participant accounts.

Employer contributions may be a percentage of salary or profits. Some of these plans also provide for employee contributions that may be voluntary or mandatory. Your retirement benefits under such a plan will be determined directly by the amount in your account when you retire. As a result, the exact amount of your retirement benefit cannot be known in advance.

The two primary types of defined contribution plans are profit-sharing and thrift plans.

Defined Benefit Plans

A defined benefit plan is set up so that the amount you will receive at retirement can be determined in advance. Your employer uses a formula to calculate what your benefit will be when you reach retirement age, usually sixty-five.

The formula is one of three general types: a flat-dollar, a career average, or a final-pay formula. Career average and final-pay formulas are most often seen in plans covering nonunion employees. Under pay-related formulas, an employer has some discretion in defining *pay* for plan purposes. The employer may choose to recognize all compensation, just your base pay, or something in between.

FINANCIAL PLANNING FOR OLDER PEOPLE

Taking good financial care of older people requires advance planning. Here are some tips. Make sure they are getting benefits they are entitled to. Check that registrations for Medicare, Social Security, and other programs are in order. If they are over sixty-five, make sure an additional exemption is taken on federal income taxes.

Older homeowners may be eligible for breaks on city and state income and property taxes. Check with the local tax assessor's office. And people over fifty-five who sell their homes are eligible for a one-time capital gains exclusion of up to $125,000. Also check with your local chapter of the American Association of Retired Persons for other programs and information that may be helpful.

Key PT

Important papers—passbooks, checking accounts, stock certificates, loan papers, and Social Security and Medicare information—should be easily located. Make sure older adults have an updated will. It may even be wise to have a living will, which specifies what kind of care they want to receive if they become very ill. (You or another person should have a copy of the living will. That way, you'll have access to it in an emergency. The original should be stored in a safe place such as a safe-deposit box.)

By helping older relatives arrange their financial affairs now, you can help them avoid costly legal and financial complications later.

INDIVIDUAL RETIREMENT ACCOUNTS

Individual retirement accounts, better known as IRAs, have been described as the tax shelter for everyone. The main attraction of the IRA is the tax shelter it provides for your money.

You can gain three tax advantages. First, you may be able to deduct from your income the full amount of your IRA contributions each year. Second, your money accumulates tax-free in an IRA. Any income and capital gains generated by your

IRA investment are not taxed until you withdraw the money. And third, by the time you begin withdrawing your IRA money at retirement, your tax bracket should be lower than it was when you earned the money.

Where to Invest Your IRA

Many financial institutions want to offer you their IRAs. They include banks, brokerage firms, credit unions, insurance companies, and mutual funds. Through these institutions, you may place a wide variety of investments in your IRA, including stocks, bonds, mutual funds, limited partnerships, annuities, and certificates of deposit. You may not, however, have precious metals or collectibles in your account.

Depending on how near you are to retirement, you should diversify your investments to provide the right proportion of growth, income, and safety.

In the early years, you can focus your objectives on growth. Later, you may want to shift funds into investments that offer a greater degree of safety.

Knowing more about retirement plans will help you prepare for a profitable and comfortable retirement.

ESTATE PLANNING

Estate planning is the process by which you prearrange your financial matters for the benefit of your family or other beneficiaries after your death.

For some, death is difficult to talk about, and estate planning discussions can become quite emotional. However, wise use of available estate planning techniques can be of considerable benefit to you by alleviating the worry of leaving a family in a state of financial hardship.

Estate planning was once regarded as the concern of only

the wealthy. That's because at one time, the primary reason for estate planning was to avoid federal estate taxes.

Today, most people should have an estate plan, regardless of the size of their estate. No matter how rich or not so rich you are, you do have an estate. It consists of all of the assets and liabilities you have at the time of your death.

One myth of estate planning is that it's for older people. Younger people actually risk more by failing to plan. Suppose you and your spouse die at the same time, leaving two young children. If you leave no will, the state will decide who raises your children.

Organizing Your Affairs

The estate planning process has six steps:

1. Organize your financial affairs.
2. Determine your total estate.
3. Identify problem areas.
4. Formulate the plan.
5. Put the plan into action.
6. Review and revise it on a regular basis.

Organizing your affairs requires that you keep information regarding your financial advisors, bank accounts, employment data, budgets, and balance sheets. In addition, insurance records, investment data, tax returns, wills, deeds, and titles to property should also be kept together.

Gather up birth, marriage, and/or divorce papers, and keep them in a safe and central location. If you organize now, you will help your loved ones by making important documents accessible after your death.

Identifying Goals

The hardest part of estate planning is identifying goals. This process will be easier if you have personal financial goals already in place.

Your estate planning goals are designed to assure that your family's financial goals remain intact. These goals may include funding retirement plans, financing a college education for your children, and providing family support should sudden death occur.

To assure a well-thought-out plan, be realistic, be complete, stay flexible, and include your family in the planning process. It is *your* life and estate, but your family will have to live with these decisions after you are gone.

The Plan

In estate planning, you may choose from several ways to achieve the same goal. To decide which alternatives are right for you, you need to know something about inflation, insurance, investments, taxes, and much more. Get the advice of an attorney, a financial planner, and specialists in life insurance, taxes, and other areas.

Once you have assembled your plan, act immediately to make sure it is carried out! Keep this plan up-to-date by revising it periodically.

Your Will

Your will is the cornerstone of your estate plan. If you die without a will, you die *intestate*. That means the state will decide how your estate is to be distributed.

The surest way to avoid problems is to make an attorney part of your estate planning team. Each state has its own peculiarities in administering or handling wills and estates.

Acceptable moves in one state—such as disinheriting a child—could be illegal in another state. Anything illegal presents grounds for challenging your entire will.

A simple will may cost several hundred dollars to draft, but done properly, it assures that your wishes are carried out after you are gone.

WILLS

Few of us like to think about death, especially our own. But if we really love our families, we'll bite the bullet and give serious thought to writing a will.

Attorneys say if you're single with no assets, a will may not be important. But if you're married or have children, you definitely need a will.

Laws regarding wills and inheritance do vary from state to state. But lawyers say in most circumstances, even when there is no dispute over property, to die intestate (without a will) is to leave a legal mess for your heirs. Without that legal document, even the simplest procedures have to be cleared by the court, costing time and money.

Will Kits

Saving money is a good idea, but not when it comes to getting a properly written will. Since probate law is very complicated, attorneys say too many things can go wrong if you try to write your will yourself. Chances are, you'll leave some things out.

In a will, it's not enough to just say who is to get what portion of your property. You must go further to give your executors the power to carry out your wishes in disposing of your property.

Some attorneys are skeptical of will kits, saying too many

variables exist in the laws from one state to another. There is no way they can all be covered in a kit.

You can expect an attorney to charge up to $500 to properly prepare a will.

Minor Children

It may seem like the best way to provide for your children's future, but listing your minor children as beneficiaries on your life insurance policy could cause major problems if you die while they are underage.

In many states, children cannot collect money without a court-appointed guardian. The guardian must be bonded, making the whole procedure expensive and complicated. Attorneys say these problems can be avoided if you make your life insurance payable to your estate. Then in your will, set up a testamentary trust for your children, thereby avoiding the need for guardianship.

A will should also stipulate who would have custody of your minor children if you die.

What to Include

A will is a tool to get a job done. That job is to clearly state what happens to your property after you are gone. But you won't be there to explain what you meant, so the will must be clearly written and should include certain stipulations.

Attorneys suggest that a will should name an executor and an alternate. If you have minor children, your will can name a guardian for them. If there is a trust for the children, the will should name a trustee.

A will should dispose of your property and give powers to the executor.

You shouldn't put funeral and burial instructions in a will since it is usually not read until *after* the funeral.

Avoid leaving specific dollar amounts to heirs because they come off the top of the estate and could leave nothing for persons farther down the list.

Where to Keep Your Will

Writing an up-to-date will is an essential part of being financially responsible. But if no one knows where your will is, it will do your heirs no good.

Lawyers say you should keep a copy of the will at home. But store the original off the premises, perhaps in a safety-deposit box. In most states, wills can be filed in the county courthouse for safekeeping.

Be sure to go back and replace the original if you make any changes in your will. Your marriage or divorce will revoke a previous will. Also, if you inherit any money, you should update your will. As a rule of thumb, review your will every three to five years.

CHOOSING YOUR FINANCIAL ADVISORS

Selecting a Financial Planner

Looking for someone to straighten out your finances? A financial planner may be just the person you need. But selecting one is no easy chore. The industry is mostly unregulated, so anyone can call himself or herself a financial planner.

Before you select a financial planner, you should check some things. Is the person qualified? A planner should be a Securities Exchange Commission (SEC)–registered investment advisor. Your planner should give you a written description of fees charged, types of clients consulted, and a summary of education and background.

Get an estimate of the costs and find out if the planner

expects to earn a commission by selling you products. Seek out and talk with two or three current clients. Examine plans prepared for these clients to see if investment recommendations are consistent with your goals.

Selecting Insurance Agents

Your insurance agent is an important player on your team of professional financial advisors. The best agent will sell you the type and amount of coverage you need. You should buy life, health, and disability insurance from a life insurance agent. If you're seeking homeowner's or auto and liability coverage, a property and casualty agent is the one you will need to consult. Most agents tend to specialize in only one group of products, so you may want to work with more than one agent.

You may not need an insurance agent at all if you know what type of insurance you want and how much you need. You can buy from some of the low-cost companies that sell by telephone. However, for most people, an insurance agent is necessary. There are two different types of agents: the direct and the independent.

Types of Agents

The agent who works for just one company is referred to as a captive agent or direct writer. This type of agent can sell insurance offered by only one company. That is fine if the company's products are competitively priced across the board, but often they are not.

Independent agents, on the other hand, work for a number of insurers. They may be able to fit you with the right coverage, or they may be promoting a company's product because it pays them a larger commission. You should base your decision on the price of the coverage and the agent's competence.

Choosing the Right Agent

Before you try to select an agent to satisfy your insurance needs, you should understand how much coverage you will need and how much it will cost you.

Get quotes from four or five agents recommended to you by friends and associates. Use these quotes to narrow down your choice of agents to two or three you feel are the most competent. Stick with agents who do most of their business with companies rated A+ in *Best's Insurance Reports*, available at your local library.

Finally, limit your list of choices to agents who have been working full-time at least four years. This work record shows a commitment to the profession. In addition, look for the following professional designations because they indicate added experience and knowledge: CPCU, for Chartered Property/Casualty Underwriter, and CLU, for Chartered Life Underwriter.

SELECTING A CHECKING ACCOUNT

In the past, banks provided the same checking and savings services to all customers, no matter how small their balances. Now, with deregulation of the banking industry, banks segment the market by separating customers according to the size of their bank balances.

Banks now seek out the more profitable, high-balance customers while discouraging not-so-profitable small accounts by applying fees and service charges.

Selecting the right checking account can save you hundreds of dollars per year. Shopping around for the best deal on a checking account is as necessary as shopping for a car. Basically, there are two types of checking accounts: those that pay interest, and those that do not.

What Type of Account Do You Have?

Noninterest-bearing accounts are referred to as regular checking. They pay no interest and may require you to pay fees. These accounts are designed for customers who maintain low balances. Expect to pay at least $3 a month plus a fee for each check if regular checking is your choice.

On the other hand, interest-bearing checking accounts include NOW accounts and Super-NOW accounts. Both pay interest. The interest on a NOW account may be set at approximately 5 to 5.50 percent, while a Super-NOW account offers an interest rate that increases as the balance increases.

Both NOW and Super-NOW accounts charge fees, which may be waived if a minimum balance is maintained. How that balance is calculated will affect the cost of the account.

Checking Account Fees and Your Balance

Banks can choose to calculate your balance in one of two ways: the low-minimum-balance or the average-daily-balance method. In the low-minimum-balance method, a fee is triggered if the balance falls below a certain amount at any time during the month. In the average-daily-balance method, a fee is activated when the monthly average of each day's balance drops below a certain dollar amount. When selecting a checking account, look for the one that uses the average-daily-balance method to calculate your balance. It is more advantageous but less common.

Your Interest Rate

Banks often boast about the high interest rates they pay on their checking accounts. But like fees, the rates depend on the amount of money in your account. The most popular methods are the tiered rate and the blended rate. The tiered rate pays the highest rate on the entire balance; the blended rate does not.

For example, a bank may pay 5 percent for balances up to $3,000 but pay 6 percent for balances $3,000 and up. If the rate was blended and you had $4,000 in the account, you would not earn 6 percent on the entire $4,000. You would earn 5 percent on the first $3,000 and 6 percent on the remaining balance. Tiered rates are preferable to blended rates.

The Best Deal for You

Here are some things to think about when shopping for the right checking account. If you write a lot of checks, a flat-fee checking account may be best for you. If you are always getting charged fees when your account falls below the minimum balance, an account with a lower minimum balance requirement would be advisable. Remember, shop around and know all the details before you make your final decision. See figure 1.10 for an easy way to compare bank checking accounts.

CHECK IT OUT

When making a purchase by check, we are often confronted with, "Do you have a major credit card?" Is this question legal? Yes, it is. Merchants may require any identification they choose before accepting a check. But you might want to check with your state authorities. Many states have passed laws prohibiting merchants from writing credit card numbers on checks. But merchants can still ask to see the card.

FIGURE 1.10

HOW TO SELECT A CHECKING ACCOUNT WORK SHEET

	Bank 1	Bank 2
Bank name	______	______
Does bank have federal deposit insurance? (yes, no)	______	______
Type of account (*write in one:* regular, NOW, Super-NOW, share draft)	______	______
Are fees charged to keep account? (*write in one:* yes; no; depends on balance)	______	______
What are the fees based on? *(check one)*		
Minimum daily balance	______	______
Average daily balance	______	______
Other	______	______
(Average daily balance is best.)		
How much are the fees for		
Monthly maintenance charges	______	______
Fees for each check written	______	______
Other fees	______	______
Interest rate paid on account balance	______	______
How is balance calculated? *(check one)*		
Average daily balance	______	______
Actual balance each day	______	______
What's the charge for		
Bouncing a check	______	______
Stopping a check payment	______	______
Printing 200 checks	______	______
Certifying a check	______	______
Making a withdrawal using		
Teller window	______	______
Bank-owned ATM	______	______

	Bank 1	Bank 2
Regional network ATM	________	________
National network ATM	________	________
Making a deposit using		
Teller window	________	________
ATM	________	________
Making a balance inquiry using		
Teller window	________	________
ATM	________	________
Extra services		
Preauthorized bill payment	________	________
Bill payment by phone	________	________
Fund transfer by phone	________	________
Signature guarantee	________	________
Balance inquiry by phone	________	________
Other factors		
Branch close to home (within 1 mile)	________	________
Branch close to office (within 1 mile)	________	________
Number of branches	________	________
Number of ATMs	________	________
Bank hours	________	________

SOCIAL SECURITY EXPLAINED

Are you suffering from social insecurity? Smart financial planning demands that you understand what benefits you should expect under Social Security. Three separate funds pay benefits under the Social Security system. The Old Age and Survivors' Insurance Trust Fund provides monthly checks to retirees, their families, and the families of deceased workers. The Disability Insurance Trust Fund pays benefits to disabled workers and their families. The Hospital Insurance Trust Fund pays Medicare claims.

Nearly everyone with earned income must pay Social Security taxes, which will someday pay benefits. The only persons exempt are some employees of federal, state, and local governments, members of the clergy who decide not to participate, and some employees of foreign companies who work outside the United States.

How to Qualify for Social Security Retirement

To qualify for retirement benefits under the Social Security system, you must have worked long enough and earned enough income to have accrued a specified number of "quarters" of Social Security coverage. Anyone fifty-nine or younger this year must have accumulated forty quarters to be eligible for benefits. That takes about ten years.

Social Security will add a quarter of coverage to your record every time your earnings reach a specified minimum level. That level rises with inflation. Currently that amount is $500. For every $500 you earn, you accrue one quarter of coverage. However, each year, you can get credit for a maximum of four quarters of coverage toward your retirement benefits.

What Happens Should You Die Unexpectedly?

Too many people think Social Security benefits only older people. However, in the event of your untimely death, there are Social Security benefits to take care of your loved ones.

Let's say you are a thirty-five-year-old man with a wife and a child. If you have accumulated at least a year and a half of earnings, your spouse and child will be eligible for survivor's benefits. Your child will receive 75 percent of your retirement benefits until age eighteen. This amount can be as much as $9,600 per year. Your wife will also get 75 percent of your benefits as long as she is caring for a child under sixteen; she can receive your full benefit when she reaches sixty-five.

In addition, your family is entitled to $250 for your funeral expenses from Social Security, regardless of your age.

How Much Have You Paid In?

The Social Security Administration will provide to you, free of charge, a statement of your earnings covered by Social Security. This statement shows your earnings history, how much you have paid in Social Security taxes, estimated future Social Security benefits, and additional information about how the program works. Contact your local Social Security Administration office and ask for Form SSA-7004 (see fig. 1.11).

THE DOLLAR SIDE OF DIVORCE

Although getting a divorce today may be less messy than it once was, it's not necessarily easier. Divorce battles of the rich and famous have always received media attention, but it might surprise you to discover that most divorcing couples settle their differences out of court.

All fifty states have no-fault divorce laws. Couples can now split up on grounds of irreconcilable differences as opposed to abandonment, mental cruelty, or adultery. The emphasis is on negotiation over assets instead of litigation over whose fault it was the marriage didn't work out.

The trend is to view marriage as a business partnership and its dissolution as the breakup of a business. Assets that were never before considered marital property are now being given a closer look, and the stakes are high. Beyond deciding the basic issues of who gets the house, the car, and the bank accounts, today's settlements often include future pension benefits, the income potential of a professional practice, or a dollar value assigned to a professional degree or license.

First, Get Help

The growing complexities of family law make it advisable for divorcing couples to negotiate using a specialist in this area. The most important step in getting a divorce is consulting a good attorney familiar with family law.

Couples should consult their own attorneys, outline the circumstances of the divorce, and list the property involved, including real estate, personal property, stocks, and bonds. List the number of children in the family, their ages, and how much it costs to maintain the household with and without children. This account will determine, in a no-fault divorce, how much child support is necessary.

Don't accept a settlement offer, even one that sounds good, without knowing all the facts. To get to the facts, your lawyer may have to subpoena your spouse's personal and business financial records, take depositions (out-of-court statements under oath), and audit tax returns.

Your lawyer must know state law, be comfortable with tax law, and know when to get help. That may mean calling in an expert such as an accountant, a financial planner, or an appraiser. Make sure you have a clear picture of the financial situation before negotiations begin.

Alimony and Child Support

Several key issues need to be resolved in the negotiation process. Two of them are alimony and child support. In the past, alimony was a long-term financial obligation paid to a woman until she either remarried or died. Nowadays, alimony is generally awarded for rehabilitative purposes. These purposes are designed to help the woman get training for employment. In a no-fault divorce with no children, alimony is rarely

Figure 1.11

SOCIAL SECURITY ADMINISTRATION REQUEST FOR EARNINGS AND BENEFIT ESTIMATE STATEMENT

The Social Security program belongs to you and you can count on it to be there for you. Social Security can protect you in many ways. It can help support your family in the event of your death and provide monthly payments and health insurance when you retire or if you become disabled.

To help you learn how Social Security is a part of your life, we are pleased to offer you a free Personal Earnings and Benefit Estimate Statement.

The Personal Earnings and Benefit Estimate Statement shows your Social Security earnings history and estimates how much you have paid in Social Security taxes. It also estimates your future benefits and tells you how you can qualify for benefits. When you receive your earnings statement, we hope you will use it to start planning for a strong financial future.

To receive your statement, please fill out the form on the reverse and mail it to us. You should receive your statement in 6 weeks or less. We look forward to sending it to you.

Gwendolyn S. King

GWENDOLYN S. KING
Commissioner of Social Security

SOCIAL SECURITY ADMINISTRATION

Request for Earnings and Benefit Estimate Statemen

To receive a free statement of your earnings covered by Social Security and your estimated future benefits, all you need to do is fill out this form. Please print or type your answers. When you have completed the form, fold it and mail it to us.

1. Name shown on your Social Security card:

   ________________ ________ ________________
   First Middle Initial Last

2. Your Social Security number as shown on your card:

   ☐☐☐-☐☐-☐☐☐☐

3. Your date of birth: _____ Month _____ Day _____ Year

4. Other Social Security numbers you have used:

   ☐☐☐-☐☐-☐☐☐☐

   ☐☐☐-☐☐-☐☐☐☐

5. Your Sex: ☐ Male ☐ Female

6. Other names you have used (including a maiden name):

   ____

   ____

7. Show your actual earnings for last year and your estimated earnings for this year. Include only wages and/or net self-employment income covered by Social Security.

   A. Last year's actual earnings:

   $☐☐☐,☐☐☐.0 0
   Dollars only

   B. This year's estimated earnings:

   $☐☐☐,☐☐☐.0 0
   Dollars only

8. Show the age at which you plan to retire: ☐☐
   (Show only one age)

Form SSA-7004-SM-OP1 (9-91) Destroy prior editions

Form Approved
OMB No. 0960-0466 SP

9. Below, show the average yearly amount that you think you will earn between now and when you plan to retire. Your estimate of future earnings will be added to those earnings already on our records to give you the best possible estimate.

Enter a yearly average, not your total future lifetime earnings. Only show earnings covered by Social Security. Do not add cost-of-living, performance or scheduled pay increases or bonuses. The reason for this is that we estimate retirement benefits in today's dollars, but adjust them to account for average wage growth in the national economy.

However, if you expect to earn significantly more or less in the future due to promotions, job changes, part-time work, or an absence from the work force, enter the amount in today's dollars that most closely reflects your future average yearly earnings.

Most people should enter the same amount that they are earning now (the amount shown in 7B).

Your future average yearly earnings:

$ ☐☐☐,☐☐☐.0 0

Dollars only

10. Address where you want us to send the statement:

Name

Street Address (Include Apt. No., P.O. Box, or Rural Route)

City State Zip Code

I am asking for information about my own Social Security record or the record of a person I am authorized to represent. I understand that if I deliberately request information under false pretenses I may be guilty of a federal crime and could be fined and/or imprisoned. I authorize you to send the statement of earnings and benefit estimates to the person named in item 10 through a contractor.

▶

Please sign your name (Do not print)

Date (Area Code) Daytime Telephone No.

ABOUT THE PRIVACY ACT

Social Security is allowed to collect the facts on this form under Section 205 of the Social Security Act. We need them to quickly identify your record and prepare the earnings statement you asked us for. Giving us these facts is voluntary. However, without them we may not be able to give you an earnings and benefit estimate statement. Neither the Social Security Administration nor its contractor will use the information for any other purpose.

We estimate that it will take you about 5 minutes to complete this form. This includes the time it will take to read the instructions, gather the necessary facts and fill out the form. If you have comments or suggestions on this estimate, or on any other aspect of this form, write to the Social Security Administration, ATTN: Reports Clearance Officer, 1-A-21 Operations Bldg., Baltimore, MD 21235, and to the Office of Management and Budget, Paperwork Reduction Project (0960-0466), Washington, D.C. 20503. **Do not send completed forms or information concerning your claim to these offices. Send them to your nearest Social Security Office.**

awarded. The judge will expect to see provisions for child support in any agreement that is submitted. In some cases, it includes private school tuition and college expenses.

Alimony can be claimed as tax-deductible, but child support cannot, nor is it included in the income of the receiving parent. Also, deciding who gets the exemption on the tax return can be resolved by signing a waiver for your ex-spouse to attach to his or her return.

Dividing Up the Property

Splitting up the property can make divorce settlements messy and expensive. In packaging divorce settlements, courts and divorcing couples have centered on the major family assets, such as the house. Traditionally, the house goes to the wife, especially if there are children, and it's common for her to get outright ownership.

Retirement benefits are often the second largest asset. Federal law allows a spouse to receive a share of benefits accrued during the marriage if a judge awards it. But you may not be willing to wait years for your share of the company pension. You might negotiate for a lump-sum payment now.

What Is Considered Marital Property?

One of the newest trends in divorce law is considering a professional degree or license marital property. Of course, that means its value can be divided in a divorce. Attorneys, doctors, and certified public accountants, among others, are the hardest hit in this area. The basic idea behind this trend is that the nonstudent spouse helped boost the future earning potential by supporting the student while he or she was in school, and therefore, the supportive spouse deserves a share of the future earnings. With long marriages, there have been cases where the court awarded the woman a percentage of the projected value of a professional license.

How Much Will It Cost?

Some divorce attorneys charge by the hour, and others have a flat fee. Make sure you find out up front how much it is going to cost. In general, a fee of $500 is reasonable for an uncontested divorce. If you can't reach an agreement outside the court, be prepared for a long, slow, and costly process of litigation that could cost $5,000 or more.

Once you and your spouse have decided on what is fair, and the settlement agreement is filed, changes are unlikely. In most cases, you can expect to have your divorce decree within thirty to sixty days.

If you need a good divorce lawyer, ask your friends and business associates for a recommendation. Or write the American Academy of Matrimonial Lawyers (20 North Michigan Avenue, Suite 540, Chicago, Illinois 60602) and ask for a list of its members in your area.

STEPFAMILY FINANCES

Managing your money can be further complicated with the added financial challenges associated with remarriage, especially when children are involved.

Not only will you now have assets and responsibilities that are "yours and mine," but you may have additional ones that include "your children" and "my children," and "your parents" and "my parents." And you have a new assortment of nieces, nephews, in-laws, ex-spouses, and their spouses.

Often, people don't have as much money to go around in the second marriage as they did in the first marriage. According to a study done at Colorado State University, remarriage will be the most common form of marriage in the 1990s.

Fewer than one-third of remarried mothers receive financial support from the children's father. Remarried couples are often reluctant to pool income and share responsibilities.

How to Budget the Money

A person who remarries after a divorce may bring a sense of distrust to the new relationship. Partners may bring unequal assets, income, and debts to the new union.

There are three ways to budget that may work in such a situation—a one-, two-, or three-account arrangement. In the one-account method, both incomes are put in one joint account, and all expenses are paid from it. With the two-account approach, couples maintain separate checking accounts from which they pay joint expenses. In a three-account situation, couples maintain separate checking accounts but also contribute to a third joint account used for shared expenses. Couples should eventually move to a one-account method for greater financial linkage and trust.

Whose Name Should the Assets Be In?

Determining who owns what and how they own it can be critical to a blended family's tax and estate planning. Joint property generally passes automatically to the surviving "joint tenant" when the spouse dies. But that may not always be desirable. For example, you own joint property with your spouse, and you die first. The property will automatically go to your spouse. When your spouse dies, the property will pass along to your spouse's family, not yours. To get around this problem, you may want to own property as "tenants in common." In that way, you can designate who should receive the property in your will.

Reviewing Your Estate

Several items need to be reviewed immediately after you remarry. They include life insurance policies, wills, bank accounts, and medical and hospital benefits.

In addition, you will want to review who is listed as beneficiary on your life insurance, pension or profit-sharing plans, and bank accounts. By taking stock of these items, you might discover that you don't have enough life insurance and/or you need to change the beneficiary.

Wills need to be updated to include your new spouse and his or her needs. Medical and hospital benefits need to be reviewed to determine if you have enough or are paying for too much coverage. Your new spouse may already have enough coverage for you and your dependents.

Reviewing your financial affairs now will save you money and time later.

THE PRICE OF PARENTING

Today's parents-to-be are generally well prepared for most aspects of "life with baby," except in one crucial area—the bills.

Most parents would agree that they need to be ready emotionally and physically for the new baby, but few new parents are ready for the financial realities that come with parenthood.

If you are a parent-to-be and have never put together a budget, now is the time to start. Total up your income. List your major expenses, separating the basics (housing, food, and installment debts) from those that are discretionary (vacations, clothing, and entertainment).

The bottom line is, if your budget is pushed to the outer

limits by maternity and baby-care costs, cut your discretionary expenses to avoid financial problems.

Expenses of Expecting

Here's what you can expect to pay out during your baby's first year. According to the Health Insurance Association of America, your obstetrician's fee will be around $1,000 and your hospital bill about $2,000. A crib, mattress, car seat, stroller, and high chair will come to about $500. After bringing the baby home, count on another $500 in additional medical costs. Add another $300 to clothe your infant. Food and formula will cost $450 but less if the mother breast-feeds. And don't forget diapers; they will cost about $600. In total, you can expect to pay more than $5,300 during your child's first year.

But you can do some things to cut your first-year expenses. Shop around for doctors and hospitals that charge lower fees. Try to negotiate with your doctor and the hospital to stretch your payments over a twelve-month period. Ask friends and relatives to pass on cribs, car seats, and other baby essentials to you, perhaps at a reduced price.

More shocking news for parents-to-be: the total cost of raising a child from birth to age eighteen—$100,000, according to the U.S. Department of Agriculture. However, if you plan, you can reduce the impact of child-rearing expenses.

YOUR KIDS' ALLOWANCES

Do children need an allowance? Some experts believe that children need their own money.

According to a recent survey, nearly half of all kids don't get an allowance. Many experts agree, however, that children should get a regular allowance to help them learn to plan by forcing them to decide between spending now or saving for later. Children need to learn to make judgments about how to spend money, and they need real money to practice with. In addition, paying an allowance can help you teach your children the basics of finance.

You can encourage your children to put part of their allowances into interest-bearing bank accounts. To open an account, most banks require at least a $50 to $100 deposit. The bank will let children open accounts if the parent cosigns.

Child psychologists agree that children should get a regular fixed allowance but differ on the issue of extra pay for extra chores. You'll have to decide that one for yourself.

How Much Should Kids Get?

The average American child between the ages of four and twelve gets $3 per week. Kids often start with $1 for allowance, then move up to $2 per week when they reach ages eight through twelve. Once kids are past age fourteen, many parents give them as much as $4 per week. Parents should keep in mind what a child's friends are getting in allowance. If you are paying less, you may want to explain why. This allowance should not include money for lunches, school supplies, or other necessities.

Don't lend allowance money before the payment date or children will learn to live on credit and not budget their money. Kids who crave expensive goodies should be encouraged to supplement their allowances with jobs.

NEW GRADS AND MONEY

Success in managing your money means starting early. If you are just graduating from high school or college, you are about to get another degree in the School of Life. This one has many degree requirements. One course that is not an elective is money management. It is part of everyone's course of study and will make the difference in whether or not you succeed in achieving your goals.

One of the first subjects you'll have to ace is *budgeting*. As a rule, plan to spend about 30 percent on housing and 15 percent on food. Keep your total debt payments, such as car loans, credit cards, and student loans, to about 25 percent. Set aside at least 5 percent for savings, and that will leave 20 percent or so for miscellaneous items—for example, entertainment, insurance, and clothing.

To keep track of things, record your daily expenses in an expense diary.

You and Your Banker

To get off on the right foot in managing your money wisely, you ought to establish a relationship with a bank. Opening a checking account is a place to start.

Students might want to consider a checking account that doesn't require a minimum balance and will charge a fee of only $3 to $5 monthly. Don't expect this type of account to pay interest.

Credit and Loans

If you have a credit card and it has a large balance, focus on paying it off before charging again. If you are a college grad, you probably have student loans. If you have loans from the federal government, you might be able to consolidate them into one and lower your monthly payments. But you will pay more in interest charges over the term.

Job Benefits

New grads starting new jobs will be faced with decisions about benefits, including health insurance and retirement plans. If your company has an employer-matched savings plan, don't waste a minute signing up. Start with an amount you know you can stick to, and increase it gradually as you get a better grip on your money.

In addition, for emergency purposes, start setting aside money in a regular bank savings account. You'll want to let it grow to an amount equal to six months of living expenses.

Be sure to sign up for health insurance coverage. Many companies don't charge for coverage for singles. Ask your parents for advice.

When completing your W-4 tax withholding form, consult your parents' accountant for advice on how to pay in only the amount you anticipate you will owe. That way, you'll keep more money in your pocket.

The New Car

An item you may be eager to buy is a car to replace that old one you've been driving around all through school. Don't act hastily. To buy a new car, you may have to come up with a 20 percent down payment. It might be a better idea to consider buying a nearly new car for less money and a lower down payment.

Check with car dealers to see if they offer price breaks to recent grads. Also, shop around for financing. Some banks offer special loan programs for new grads.

When selecting car insurance, start with your parents' agent. But be prepared for a shock. Insurance can be expensive, and men will pay more than women. Shop around and compare prices. Inquire about the discounts the insurance company may offer.

The Apartment

Graduating from high school or college is a happy occasion. But moving out on your own and finding out what apartments rent for can be discouraging. You thought you might get rid of roommates when you graduated. Think again. In most American cities, apartments can cost $500 and up monthly.

If you decide on a roommate or roommates, make sure all of your names appear on the lease and any other documents you may have to sign. That way, you won't be held solely responsible if there is a problem down the road.

Be sure to set some ground rules. Is smoking allowed? Who pays what bills?

A one- or two-year lease will be most advisable. It will lock you in with a predictable rent payment. Also, look into rental insurance to cover your personal belongings. Make sure the policy reimburses you for replacement cost instead of actual cash value.

THE BEST DAY CARE

Choosing the right day care affects your child and your budget. Day-care centers are often a must for working parents. Locating high-quality care to fit your budget and serve your needs and your child's can be challenging. Here are some guidelines to help.

Find out what services are available in your community by checking with your state's child-care licensing agency, which might be listed in the phone book under the Department of Human Services, Social Services, or Health.

Also, get suggestions from relatives, friends, and coworkers. You might want to check the phone book for the local chapter of the National Child Care Association and ask for a referral.

What to Expect

You can choose from a broad variety of child-care centers. Settings range from private homes to large day-care centers. To begin the screening process, look first at licensed child-care centers.

In most states, any place that keeps three or four unrelated children is required to be licensed. But be careful. Licensing and registration requirements vary from state to state. Just because a child-care center is licensed does not necessarily mean it provides quality care.

Check with your state's child-care licensing agency to find out about licensing requirements. In addition, the agency may be able to provide you with a checklist for evaluating child care. But don't rule out unlicensed day care; it may be an excellent alternative.

The Cost

The price of day care can vary greatly. Family day care, where children are kept in the home, can cost from $35 to $160 per child per week. In day-care centers, cost for the same care can range from $60 to $150.

Most family day care is less expensive than day-care centers. Expensive day care does not necessarily mean better quality. Remember, costs are tied to the overhead the center has to maintain, which includes teacher salaries and rent or mortgage costs. These variables have more to do with the location of the center than the quality of the care. Make sure the child-care provider you select will allow you to drop in unannounced.

YOUR FAITH AND YOUR FINANCES

Many churches are offering members a variety of support groups, programs, and seminars to help them cope in our complex society. One topic that is becoming popular is personal finance. Churches around the country are teaching biblically based principles related to money management.

The Bible has hundreds of verses that deal with handling money. Subjects covered include debt, investing, budgets, insurance, charitable giving, and teaching children wise money management skills. Many people are turning to the Scriptures, looking for sound advice that is divinely inspired.

Dealing with Debt

Many people are struggling with debt. Can we find biblical guidelines? There are many warnings about the misuse of debt. The Bible never mentions that debt is wrong or sinful, but it cautions that debt is a kind of slavery and that being overextended without a means for repayment can mean the loss of your possessions and, more important, your reputation. One clear direction is given: that is, if you borrow money, you must repay it. The biblical financial advice shared is that declaring bankruptcy is not an alternative to working out a plan with your creditors.

Saving and Investing

Saving and investing are areas of much concern for many people. Of course, the Bible encourages saving money on a regular basis, and the recommended amount is 20 percent! This amount is revealed in Genesis 41:34.

Some basic advice from the Scriptures involve diversification—spreading your money among different types of investments because you never know which investment will prove profitable. The Bible also warns against investing in speculative get-rich-quick schemes; it's wiser to put your money in investments you are familiar with.

Charitable Giving

What does the Bible say about giving to the poor? You probably remember from Sunday school the verse, "It is more blessed to give than to receive." In the biblical sense, giving is recognized as an admission that a higher authority governs the universe. Giving to support the work of the church and those who are less fortunate is an acknowledgment of that divine influence.

In addition, when we give, we in turn receive a blessing equal to or greater than the gift. Stewardship over finances is a constant theme in the Bible, and a closer examination will unfold principles that you can apply to your financial life today.

Insurance

Is insurance Bible based? Insurance deals with *restitution*, which literally means "to restore." In the area of finances, this term normally refers to replacing a material possession. In the books of Exodus, Leviticus, and Deuteronomy, verses touch on subjects as diverse as payment for theft and responsibility for borrowed goods. And the book of Proverbs discusses leaving an inheritance for your children. Not only does the Bible advise that we leave money to our children, but it goes further to imply that we should give some of the inheritance while we are still alive to teach the children how to manage it.

THE BUSINESS OF BANKING

Money! We all use it, but what is it really? Basically, money is anything we can use to make purchases. By law currency, or cash, is money, and a seller must accept it as payment. A check, however, is not cash and does not have to be accepted for payment, even though it is the most frequently used method of payment.

In the past, items such as whale teeth and tobacco have been used as money. But whether money is numbers on a computer printout or pieces of paper with pictures on them, behind all symbols rests the central requirement of faith. Money serves its purpose only as long as we believe in it.

Money has been called "the promises men live by." But you don't keep all of your money with you at all times. You keep it in a bank. Where does the bank keep its money?

The Bankers' Bank

The Federal Reserve Bank, or the Fed as it is often called, is charged with the responsibility of controlling the flow of money throughout our economy. One of its most important functions is to establish reserve requirements, that is, the amount of money that banks have to keep at the Fed at all times. It is expressed as a percentage, which can be as high as 18 percent or as low as 1 percent, depending on whether the deposit is for checking or savings. So, for example, a bank may have to keep 10 percent of the total deposits for all of its checking accounts in cash at the Fed.

What does the bank do with the rest of the money? The bank can loan it to consumers and businesses and use it to make investments in corporate or government bonds. That is how the bank earns an income.

To make a profit, the bank must make sure the difference between the interest it pays out on deposits and the interest it brings in on loans is adequate. For example, the bank may have to pay 5 percent interest on deposits but may lend the money for 10 percent. After subtracting expenses for salaries and overhead, the bank may earn a 2 percent profit on each deposit.

In other words, banking is a business, one that can be profitable and can fuel the growth of the nation.

PLANNING PERKS

Some employers offer financial planning as a benefit. A recent survey by a benefits planning firm found that 11 percent of the 411 companies made arrangements for financial planning for employees. Of those that do not currently grant the benefit, 35 percent plan to introduce it.

Financial planning was once offered only to a company's senior management. But now employers want to educate their employees about how investments work and how to get the most out of the company benefits. Employers realize that employees who feel confident about their finances will make better employees. Companies often sponsor one-day seminars, on company time, to which all employees and their spouses are invited.

2

INVESTING

SAVING YOUR MONEY

How much do you save on a regular basis? Some people don't save. It's not because they don't want to save; the reason lies closer to not knowing how and in what amounts to save. A good rule of thumb is to save 10 percent of your monthly gross income. But, if you can't handle 10 percent, why not 2 or 5 percent or whatever you can afford? You should start now and be consistent. The earlier you start saving, the better (see fig. 2.1).

The more you save, the easier it becomes and the faster you will meet your goals. For instance, if your monthly gross income is $1,000 and you save just 10 percent, that will equal $100 each month, or $1,200 per year plus interest.

Now, saving isn't easy and requires you to use some discipline, but you can do it. Your future depends on it.

How to Save

Saving money is like having insurance. You don't realize it's important until you need it. When you think about a savings plan, the first type that comes to mind is making a regular deposit to your savings account. This method may be one of the most common, but it's not the most popular.

FIGURE 2.1

SAVINGS ACCUMULATION WORK SHEET

Time is an element we cannot control, other than to start saving now. Answer this question: Who do you think would accumulate more by age sixty-five? A person who started to save $1,000 a year at age twenty-one, saved for eight years, and then completely stopped? Or a person who saved $1,000 a year for thirty-seven years who started at age twenty-nine? Both earned 10 percent on their savings. Is it the person who saved a total of $8,000 or the one who saved $37,000? Study the chart below.

	Individual A		Individual B	
Age	**Contribution**	**Year-End Value**	**Contribution**	**Year-End Value**
21	1,000	1,100	0	0
22	1,000	2,310	0	0
23	1,000	3,641	0	0
24	1,000	5,105	0	0
25	1,000	6,716	0	0
26	1,000	8,487	0	0
27	1,000	10,436	0	0
28	1,000	12,579	0	0
29	0	13,837	1,000	1,100
30	0	15,221	1,000	2,310
31	0	16,743	1,000	3,641
32	0	18,417	1,000	5,105
33	0	20,259	1,000	6,716
34	0	22,284	1,000	8,487
35	0	24,513	1,000	10,436

	Individual A		Individual B	
Age	**Contribution**	**Year-End Value**	**Contribution**	**Year-End Value**
36	0	26,964	1,000	12,579
37	0	29,661	1,000	14,937
38	0	32,627	1,000	17,531
39	0	35,889	1,000	20,384
40	0	39,478	1,000	23,523
41	0	43,426	1,000	26,975
42	0	47,769	1,000	30,772
43	0	52,546	1,000	34,950
44	0	57,800	1,000	39,545
45	0	63,580	1,000	44,599
46	0	69,938	1,000	50,159
47	0	76,932	1,000	56,275
48	0	84,625	1,000	63,003
49	0	93,088	1,000	70,403
50	0	103,397	1,000	78,543
51	0	112,636	1,000	87,497
52	0	123,898	1,000	97,347
53	0	136,290	1,000	108,182
54	0	149,919	1,000	120,100
55	0	164,911	1,000	133,210
56	0	181,402	1,000	147,631
57	0	199,542	1,000	163,494
58	0	219,496	1,000	180,943
59	0	241,446	1,000	200,138
60	0	265,590	1,000	221,252
61	0	292,149	1,000	244,477
62	0	321,364	1,000	270,024
63	0	353,501	1,000	298,127
64	0	388,851	1,000	329,039
65	0	427,736	1,000	363,043
Total Investment		**$8,000**	**Total Investment**	**$37,000**
Total Amount Accumulated		**$427,736**	**Total Amount Accumulated**	**$363,043**

Many people have found it much easier to save by payroll deduction—having the employer deduct a fixed amount from the paycheck each pay period and applying it to a designated savings vehicle. This method is popular because it gets the money out of your hands before you spend it. If your employer doesn't have a payroll deduction plan, many banks will draft your checking account each month and deposit it in a savings account. But if you want to write a check to deposit in your savings account, make sure it is the first check you write when you sit down to pay your bills. It may be difficult, but the saving habit is its own reward.

Creating a Cash Reserve

Saving money consistently will prepare you for investing. A cash reserve is the foundation of any financial plan (see fig. 2.2). The main benefit of your cash reserve is that you earn a safe and guaranteed return and the funds can be converted to cash without a penalty or loss of principal. Your total cash reserve should be equal to at least six months' expenses. If your monthly expenses total $1,000, your cash reserve should amount to at least $6,000.

Why a cash reserve? It gives you an immediate supply of hard cash to cover monthly expenses in the event of an emergency. The money to build your cash reserve will come from your regular savings plan. That's the 5 or 10 percent of your monthly gross income you promised to set aside on a regular basis. Creating a cash reserve will take some discipline, but it is the foundation of your investment program and will protect you from financial hardship.

Types of Savings Accounts

What type of savings account is best for you? Having a knowledgeable bank representative to consult with will save you money. By outlining your investment objectives and seeking advice, your alternatives will be clearer, and you can make choices.

Your investment objectives for your six-month cash reserve must be safe and easily converted to cash. For starters, you will need a money market account. This account will allow you to make deposits and withdrawals without a penalty. Keep the equivalent of three months' expenses in this account.

A certificate of deposit, commonly called a CD, is a redeemable bond issued by a bank with maturities from ninety days to five years. Keep an amount equal to three months' expenses in this type of account with a maturity of not more than three months. A savings account and a CD are important tools for building your cash reserve fund.

Compound vs. Simple Interest

Benjamin Franklin wrote, "Money can earn money, and its offspring can earn more." Once you start comparing savings accounts, you'll discover that the interest rate can be calculated several ways. The interest rate you receive on your money is as significant as how often the interest is compounded.

Compound interest is the method by which your interest earns interest. Simple interest means you don't receive interest on your interest, only on the principal, the original amount you deposited.

For example, $1,000 compounded monthly at 9 percent will grow to $1,309 in three years. The same at 9 percent simple interest will grow to only $1,270, a difference of almost $40. The advantage of compound interest is even more evident with larger amounts. It is equally important for you to know how often your interest is being compounded—yearly, quarterly, monthly, or daily. Don't be afraid to ask questions about your money. Make sure you know all the details.

INVESTING YOUR MONEY

Are you a saver or an investor? There is a difference.

A saver tries to preserve and keep the money safe. A saver looks for financial vehicles that are guaranteed. He is more concerned with getting his original investment back. He wants to be sure that when he wants his money, it will be there.

An investor puts the money at risk to achieve a higher financial return. An investor commits money to an investment where the return is not guaranteed or very safe. When it is time to cash in the investment, she may receive more or less than she put in. The investor realizes that what she gives up in safety, she may get back many times in higher returns.

People with financial savvy save a certain amount of money and invest a separate amount.

Building an Investment Fund

Beginning an investment fund is the key to building wealth (see fig. 2.2). Once you have enough in your savings to pay all your bills and expenses for six months, you have satisfied the requirements of your cash reserves, and it's time to start your investment fund. The money for your investment fund will come from your regular savings pledge and any excess you have accumulated in your cash reserve fund.

The goal for your investment fund will be to earn higher yields than could be attained through a regular savings account. In addition, you must be willing to accept a slightly higher degree of risk in exchange for a higher return.

Money invested will be divided into two categories—*appreciation* and *income*. Appreciation or growth investments include growth stocks and real estate. Income investments are centered mostly on different types of bonds and some stocks.

Figure 2.2

PREPARING FOR INVESTING

Cash Reserve Fund

Purpose: To have savings equal to six months of your expenses invested in cash or its equivalent.

Goals: Very safe
Guaranteed rate of return
Easily converted to cash (easy to withdraw)

Portfolio Mix: Three months' expenses invested in safe interest-bearing account
Example: Insured money market account

Three months' expenses invested in cash equivalents
Examples: Certificates of deposit or treasury bills that mature in three months

Liquidity Reserve

Purpose: To provide a second level of security by having 5 percent of your net worth or an additional six months' expenses invested.

Goals: A higher yield than in cash reserve fund
Higher degree of risk
Easily converted to cash

Portfolio Mix: Diversification is the key. Allocate money depending on risk tolerance.

Examples: Mutual funds—bond or stock funds
Stocks rated A or better
Bonds rated BBB or better

Optional Investment Fund

Purpose: To invest in higher yielding and riskier investments that will produce greater investment results.

Goals: Investments with higher returns
A more aggressive stance with investments

Portfolio Mix: Diversification is important. Allocate money depending on risk tolerance.

Examples: Aggressive growth mutual funds
Aggressive growth stocks
High-yield bond funds
High-yield bonds
Gold
Real estate
Collectibles
Owning a business

Risk and Return

The return on your investment should outweigh the risk. If you are prepared to accept greater risk, you may achieve even higher returns on your investments. The relationship between risk and return does not mean that you will always earn higher returns on your investments by taking greater risks. But if there is a high degree of risk, you should expect a higher return.

Risk involves the possibility of loss. All investments have some degree of risk. Risk focuses on the future and the ability to forecast results based on past experiences.

A basic rule of investing is to never invest more than you can afford to lose. Persons who are risk takers in life tend to go for the higher risks in their investments.

Diversification

Don't put all your eggs in one basket! The most important reason for diversification is to spread out the risk. An investment that seems best for you today may not be best next month or next year. As a wise investor, you should purchase several investments that together will meet your needs and outperform the average. That way, you spread out or reduce the risk.

Make it a habit to review your investments quarterly. If certain economic assumptions have changed since your last evaluation, you may want to alter your investment strategy.

When making decisions about investments, you will not always be right. Diversification will give you some insurance.

INVESTING IN BONDS

A bond is an IOU or promissory note. When you buy a bond, the issuer promises to repay the principal you have loaned him or her on a specific date. In the meantime, interest is paid twice a year at a fixed annual rate set when the bonds were first offered for sale.

Bondholders have first access to the company's assets in case of bankruptcy because the assets usually serve as collateral for the bonds. This policy makes bonds a much safer investment than stocks. However, bondholders are not owners of the company and will not participate in increased earnings or in the growth of the company.

Bond-rating agencies, such as Moody's and Standard & Poor's, judge the creditworthiness of companies issuing the bonds. This evaluation is similar to a credit check made by a bank for a consumer loan. Companies with the best ratings can issue bonds at lower interest rates.

Should You Invest in Bonds?

Bonds have been the traditional counterpart to common stocks in a balanced investment portfolio. But bonds have their advantages and disadvantages.

On the positive side, the interest rate on a bond is fixed and is paid twice a year. And if you buy municipal bonds, the interest is free of federal and sometimes state income taxes. The principal on your bonds will be repaid at a set maturity date. You can even use bonds as collateral for a loan.

But here are some drawbacks of bond investing. The market value of your bonds can fluctuate with changes in interest rates. The interest rate on bonds is fixed and will not change over the years. An interest rate that looks attractive now may not be so in later years.

Municipal Bonds

You can save money on your taxes by investing in municipal bonds. They are bonds issued by local governments, cities, states, and counties. Munis, as they are often referred to, offer interest free of federal income tax. Most states also allow the income to be exempt from state and local taxes if the bonds are issued locally.

The after-tax yield on municipal bonds may be even greater than the yield you receive on taxable investments such as savings accounts. Let's see how this works. A municipal bond that pays interest at 7 percent is equivalent to an investor in the 28 percent tax bracket earning almost 10 percent on a taxable investment.

Buying municipal bonds can help you achieve better after-tax yields. Remember, it's not what you earn that's important; it's what you get to keep.

Corporate Bonds

Corporate bonds offer not only generous yields but price stability as well. Corporations issue bonds to finance their various projects. The two major types of corporate bonds are mortgage obligations and debentures.

Mortgage obligation bonds are backed by a lien on property—a factory, a power plant, or an airplane. Debentures, on the other hand, are guaranteed only by the promise of the company to repay the money and are not backed by any specific assets.

To help investors judge the financial soundness of a company, corporate bonds are given ratings that range from D to AAA (the highest) by Moody's and Standard & Poor's. These ratings measure the safety of interest and principal payments and are not to be used as recommendations to buy or sell.

Government Bonds

If safety is your primary investment objective, government bonds are the best investment for you. These bonds are the responsibility of the U.S. government, which guarantees their principal and interest.

Series EE bonds are sold at a discount from face value and pay full value at maturity. Series HH bonds earn interest twice a year. They are purchased at face value and are available only through conversion of Series EE bonds.

There are three basic types of treasury securities. *Treasury bills* are issued at a discount from face value with maturities of ninety-one days to one year, with a minimum investment of $10,000. *Treasury notes* have a fixed maturity of one to ten years and pay interest twice a year. *Treasury bonds* are similar to treasury notes but have maturities of more than ten years and higher yields. Notes and bonds require a $1,000 minimum investment.

ZERO COUPON BONDS

Zero coupon bonds may be your ticket to a comfortable retirement for you or a college education for the kids. They have become one of the more popular investment products introduced in recent years.

To many investors, they are better known by the names used by investment firms that repackage treasury securities: CATS, for certificates of accrual on treasury securities, and TIGRS, for treasury investment growth receipts.

The term *zero coupon* is used because the interest has been separated from the principal on these bonds, and there are no coupons to clip. With regular bonds, you periodically detach coupons to obtain interest from them.

You buy zero coupon bonds at a deep discount—anywhere from 20 to 90 percent of their face value. At maturity, you receive the full face value of the bonds. The return you get is the difference between the price you pay for the bonds and the face value. The interest accrues each year, but you receive it only at maturity.

Advantages of Zeros

Several advantages have made zero coupon bonds popular investments. They offer convenience; you don't have to remember to clip coupons to receive your interest.

You don't have to worry about reinvesting the interest income as it accrues. In addition, you know from the outset what return the investment will provide and how much you will receive at maturity.

Zero coupon bonds also provide you with much-needed flexibility for investment planning. You can select a maturity date for a zero that will meet the specific cash needs you anticipate, whether six months or thirty years down the road, such as a second home, retirement, or a college education for your children.

Different Types of Zeros

Zero coupon bonds come in a variety of forms. Zeros that are backed by treasury bonds are packaged as CATS, TIGRS, STRIPS, and various other names. Treasury-backed zeros provide excellent security since they represent obligations of the U.S. Treasury. Corporations and municipal governments also issue zeros. Tax-exempt municipal bond zeros are gaining in popularity and may provide a good choice for high-tax bracket investors. Zero coupon municipal bonds may offer investors a better way to reach their objectives than with traditional tax-free, fixed-income investments.

Imagine you need $100,000 in twenty-five years when you retire. Simply invest $20,000 in zero coupon bonds, maturing at that time, selling at about $200 each. In this example, your tax-free capital gain would be equal to five times your original investment.

Remember this: when interest rates are falling, the price (how much you paid) of your bond will rise; when interest rates are rising, the price of your bond will fall.

WALL STREET TALK

Traders on Wall Street, like people in any profession, have their own jargon, a specialized vocabulary that gives new meaning to certain words.

Take the terms *bull* and *bear* market. What do these words mean? *Bear* is shorthand for pessimism or a decline in growth. *Bull*, on the other hand, refers to optimism or growth in the economy.

A person who is bullish believes securities prices will rise. A bear thinks prices will fall. Bear markets often follow bad economic news.

If you play the Wall Street game, you need not be one way or the other. You can be bullish on stocks in general but bearish on steel stocks.

To determine what investments to make, you would be wise to first decide in which direction the economy is moving, bullish (which is up) or bearish (which is down).

What Is a Load?

When investing in mutual funds, you will find that they are separated into two different groups—load funds and no-load funds. Loads are the sales fees charged by the fund and paid to the broker or financial planner who sells you the shares in the fund. The two types of mutual funds are discussed later in this chapter.

What Is the Dow?

The Dow is the nickname for the Dow Jones Industrial Average of thirty major stocks (see fig. 2.3). The Dow is the most widely quoted economic measurement. It is believed to be a symbol of the rise and fall of stock prices, and it offers an indication of how the economy is doing in general.

Knowing how much the Dow goes up or down on any given day is less important than knowing what the trend is. One way to use the Dow is as an aid in evaluating your stock's performance. If the Dow rose 20 percent one year and your stock rose only 10 percent, you know your stock underperformed the market. You may want to consider selling your stock, changing your broker, or revising your investment strategy.

Figure 2.3

DOW JONES INDUSTRIAL AVERAGE (DJIA)
DJIA THIRTY COMPONENTS

Company	Symbol	Company	Symbol
Allied-Signal Inc.	ALD	Int'l Business Machines	IBM
Aluminum Co. of America	AA	International Paper	IP
American Express	AXP	J. P. Morgan & Co.	JPM
American Tel. & Tel.	T	McDonald's Corp.	MCD
Bethlehem Steel	BS	Merck & Co.	MRK
Boeing Co.	BA	Minnesota Mining & Mfg.	MMM
Caterpillar Inc.	CAT	Philip Morris	MO
Chevron Corporation	CHV	Procter & Gamble	PG
Coca-Cola Co.	KO	Sears Roebuck	S
DuPont (E. I.)	DD	Texaco, Inc.	TX
Eastman Kodak	EK	Union Carbide	UK
Exxon Corp.	XON	United Technologies	UTX
General Electric	GE	Walt Disney Co.	DIS
General Motors	GM	Westinghouse Electric	WX
Goodyear Tire	GT	Woolworth Corp.	Z

Buying Stocks Over the Counter

There are 1,600 stocks listed on the New York Stock Exchange, and another 1,100 on the American Stock Exchange. These numbers are dwarfed by the 20,000 stocks listed on the over-the-counter market, or OTC.

The primary OTC market is known as the National Association of Securities Dealers Automated Quotations System, or NASDAQ. This system offers a computer and telephone communications network that connects brokers who represent buyers and sellers all over the country. This system is so efficient it rivals the New York Stock Exchange in importance.

Many major companies choose to sell their securities over the counter. The OTC market refers to the times when some stocks had to be purchased at the offices of brokers or banks, literally over the counter.

OWNING A PIECE OF AMERICA

Buying and selling stock is a way to own part of America. The purchase or sale of stock is really a simple process. You will, however, have to enlist the help of a stockbroker to complete the transaction.

After you place your order with your broker, if it's a stock on the New York Stock Exchange, the broker wires it to the exchange. The price is then negotiated and relayed back to your broker for confirmation.

Brokers charge a fee or commission to handle the transaction. The fee is determined by the number of shares you are buying and the price of the stock.

Stocks are usually bought and sold in groups of one hundred, called round lots. You can buy three or four shares, but the price may be higher. Stock bought in an amount less than one hundred is called an odd lot.

INVESTING IN STOCKS

In general, businesses are organized as a sole proprietorship, a partnership, or a corporation. But only corporations are allowed to issue stocks and bonds.

A corporation is a legal entity apart from its owners, the shareholders. It can own property in its own name, incur debts, and sue and be sued. This separate existence means shareholders are in a position of limited liability.

If the corporation can't pay its debts, no shareholder has to. The corporation can simply declare bankruptcy. But in a partnership or sole proprietorship, the personal assets of the owners can be taken and used to satisfy any debt that the company incurs.

All corporations have stock. One type is called common; the other type is called preferred.

Common Stock

When you own common stock, you have certain rights as a shareholder in a corporation. These rights include the right to vote and elect directors of the company, the right to receive your share of profits in the form of dividends, and the right to receive a copy of the corporation's annual report.

As a common stockholder, you don't have first claim on the assets and earnings of the company. That privilege is reserved for creditors, bondholders, and preferred stockholders.

Common stock offers you the best possibility of growth, and most experts consider it to be a hedge against inflation. Investing in common stocks offers you an excellent opportunity to participate in the growth of a company and the nation's economy but is riskier than investing in preferred stocks or bonds.

Preferred Stock

Does *preferred* mean "better"? It doesn't necessarily. The word *preferred* relates to having priority over the common stockholders when it comes to the distribution of dividends and assets in the event of the breakup of a corporation.

Preferred stock is a cross between stocks and bonds. The dividend yield is fixed and limited, and preferred stock has no maturity. Shareholders with this type of stock are considered owners of the corporation, just like common shareholders, but preferred shareholders generally don't have voting rights.

Many investors buy preferred stock for the steady income it offers and the hope that their principal will increase over the years. Although growth possibilities with preferred stocks are not as good as with common stocks, preferred stocks are usually an appropriate vehicle for protecting your original investment, except during severe inflationary periods.

Why Invest in Stocks?

Historically, stocks have been one of the top investments. The Center for Research in Security Prices at the University of Chicago has conducted studies on stock market prices since 1926. One of their most significant findings disclosed that if an investor had chosen any stock at random, and had bought and sold that stock at random over a period from 1926 to 1960, the person would have made a profit 78 percent of the time.

The average return on the investment, assuming the person reinvested all dividends paid on the stock, would have been 9.8 percent a year. These are considered spectacular findings since Americans went through a depression and a major world war during that time period.

Even though the economic outlook may seem uncertain, the potential for above-average returns will always remain in the stock market.

PROFITS IN STOCKS

How do you know a stock with real growth potential when you see one? Compared to bonds, which are designed to pay a fixed amount of interest, the return on a common stock investment can be hard to predict. However, many useful methods estimate what kind of return a stock is likely to produce. These methods draw on a wide range of information, including economic data, the interest rate outlook, industry trends, and world events. Equally important, stock selection requires a close look at a corporation's financial history, its current business, and its prospects for the future.

When buying stocks, most investors turn to the ratings and recommendations compiled by analysts at investment firms and investment publications.

How the Economy Affects Stocks

Ironically, a rapidly growing economy can be bad for stocks. The level of growth expected for the economy and interest-rate forecasts influence the outlook for stock performance. In a growing economy—measured by such indicators as new housing starts, retail sales, and industrial production—corporate profits often rise. These increased profits, or expected increases in profits, can push stock prices up.

If the economy grows too quickly and "overheats," demand for money to fund expansion can shoot up and produce higher interest rates. These higher rates reduce corporate profits because of the higher cost of borrowing. In addition, higher interest rates can drive investors away from stocks and into money markets and other fixed-income investments.

In Which Industries Should You Buy Stocks?

You should consider three broad categories of industry groups.

Defensive industries tend to offer stability, weathering poor economic conditions better than other types of industries. Food and drug companies and utilities fall into this category.

Cyclical industries, unlike defensive industries, tend to fare poorly during economic downturns but blossom with an expanding economy. Companies in the steel, automotive, paper, and housing industries are good examples.

Growth industries are expanding, typically because of a growing demand for goods or services produced by the industry. Examples today include robotics, health care, and computer services. Companies in growth industries provide stockholders with greater potential for profit.

Rating the Performance of a Stock

A stock analyst devotes a large segment of time to looking at the past, present, and future performance of individual companies and their stock.

As a stockholder, you can collect profits through dividend payments, growth in the value of your stock, or both. There are two ways of measuring your return—the dividend yield and the earnings yield.

The dividend yield is obtained by dividing the dividend payout by the price of the stock. Instead of paying dividends, some companies plow all earnings back into operations. This method increases the companies' profits and, they hope, the stock price. Because of this, additional measures are used to size up stocks.

The earnings yield, determined by dividing the stock price by earnings, shows what a company is earning in relation to the price of the stock.

This same basic information is sometimes called the price/earnings ratio, or multiple. For example, a company may earn $2 per share and sell at $30 per share. The price/earnings ratio (P/E as it is sometimes referred to) is fifteen, that is, thirty divided by two.

A high P/E ratio shows investor enthusiasm in the prospects for the stock. A low P/E ratio may mean that the stock has been spurned by investors or that the stock's potential is not widely recognized.

This approach to stock evaluation is called fundamental analysis. It includes an evaluation of a company's assets, profits, management, and products.

DIVIDEND REINVESTMENT PLANS

Looking for ways to invest in the stock market? How would you like to invest in solid Fortune 500 companies conveniently and inexpensively? Dividend reinvestment plans may just fill the bill.

As the name indicates, dividend reinvestment plans allow you to reinvest your dividends automatically in additional shares in the company. The advantages of this plan include no brokerage commissions and not a lot of money to get started. If the company has a stock purchase plan, you may also be able to purchase stock directly from the company, often at a reduced cost.

To get started, you must purchase one share of stock from a

stockbroker, then have the stock registered in your name and mailed to you. When you receive the stock certificate, request information on the company's dividend reinvestment plan. A list of more than seven hundred firms that offer reinvestment plans is available for $2 from the Standard & Poor's Corp., 25 Broadway, New York, New York 10004. Or you can call your local stockbroker for more information.

INVESTING IN MUTUAL FUNDS

Investing in mutual funds can be a safe and convenient way to invest in stocks or bonds. A mutual fund is a type of investment group set up to invest for a specific purpose. Basically, here's how a mutual fund works. A number of investors pool their money, determine an investment objective, and invest the money in a group of stocks or bonds that will achieve that objective.

They may invest in securities that are designed to achieve growth, income, or both. Each investor in the fund receives a certain amount of shares in proportion to the money invested. The day-to-day value of the shares is calculated by dividing the total value of the securities by the number of shares outstanding on that day. The resulting figure is called the net asset value. The net asset value will go up or down depending on whether the stocks or bonds in the fund rise or fall.

Why Invest in a Mutual Fund?

The main reason is that you can make money with mutual funds. The average growth fund has averaged about 13 percent a year from 1987 through 1991. But some funds have gained as much as 100 percent a year. Not bad! Also, mutual funds can be bought for small or large amounts of money. Some funds will accept an initial investment of only $250.

Investors like mutual funds because they offer diversification and the opportunity to invest in a fund that suits almost any investment objective.

Funds offer professional management for people who want to invest in the stock market but are too busy to manage their money on a day-to-day basis. You can easily get your money out of a fund or exchange it with other funds. Mutual funds are a smart investment for retirement plans.

How to Select a Mutual Fund

You can choose from more than one thousand mutual funds. The first step in selecting a mutual fund is to define your investment objectives for the next several years. Are you looking for growth, income, or just a parking place for extra cash?

Talk with a stockbroker or consult such sources as *Forbes* magazine's annual mutual fund survey or *Money* magazine to determine which mutual funds are available.

When you compare the performance of a fund, look for a good track record over a five- to ten-year period.

What Type of Fund for You?

Mutual fund objectives fall into several groups. Some growth funds seek capital gains rather than income. Their main objective is to increase the value of the shares by investing in common stocks. Income funds, on the other hand, seek income for their shareholders by investing mostly in bonds. Balanced funds try to get the best of both worlds. They split their assets between stocks and bonds.

Money market funds have also become popular with investors. They enable you to invest money for short periods of time with no penalty for early withdrawal.

Should You Pay a Sales Charge?

Mutual funds are usually operated by management companies and sold through fund distributors. The fund is sold by a direct sales force, through the mail, or by a stockbroker. As previously stated, there are two main types—no-load and load funds.

A load fund charges the buyer a sales commission based on the amount of the purchase. The commission may run as high as 8 percent or more. Load funds are sold through salespeople, like stockbrokers.

A no-load fund charges no sales commission but may charge a small withdrawal fee. No-load funds are sold through advertising.

As an example of the difference between the two types of mutual funds, a $1,000 investment buys $1,000 worth of no-load fund shares but only $915 worth of shares in a fund with an 8.5 percent load.

Do load funds outperform no-load funds? Not necessarily. In the past, there has been no direct correlation between the load paid and the performance of the fund. So always consider a no-load fund when you invest in mutual funds. Just remember that since no-load funds have no sales force, you will have to do your own research to select the one that is right for you.

HOW TO INVEST

If you put $100 a month into a savings account earning 5.5 percent, after twenty years you would have put aside $24,000, and your account would be worth more than $43,000. Not bad. But if you put that same $100 per month into something that earned 12.5 percent (about what a conservative growth mutual fund earns long term), your account would be worth $107,000.

With these kinds of yields, no wonder investing looks like more fun than saving. But the bigger the potential reward, the greater the risk of losing instead of making money.

Before jumping into investing, you need to know how to invest. These two rules may help: never invest in something you don't understand, and always figure out precisely under what conditions you will sell an investment.

The Pyramid

To take the plunge and start investing, you need to be aware of how to stay afloat. One technique that investors use is called the pyramid of risk approach.

The pyramid model is built on the idea that your investment portfolio should have the right balance of safe, income, and growth investments. At the foundation of the pyramid are safe, secure investments. As you move up the pyramid, the level of risk increases. By using this method, you divide up your portfolio according to your investment profile.

If you're young and just starting to invest, you might put 60 percent or more of your assets in growth investments like stocks and split up the rest among investments whose objectives are income and safety.

Safe Investments

The safe portion of your investment portfolio provides the basis for your financial strength. Your main objective here is preservation of capital.

Investments in this category include certificates of deposit, available at your local bank or savings and loan. They are issued with maturities of three months to five years or longer.

They usually pay interest on a monthly or quarterly basis with a stiff penalty if you cash them in before maturity.

Other safe investments include treasury bills, which are guaranteed by the government and issued at a discount. They are available in $10,000 minimum amounts from the U.S. Treasury and pay interest at maturity in three-month, six-month, or one-year terms.

Treasury notes and bonds are also appropriate; they require a minimum investment of $1,000. They have maturities from one to thirty years and pay interest semiannually.

Income Investments

Many conservative investors want more than just safety from their investments. They want safe investments, but they also want high current income. The investor may be a retiree living on a pension and needing additional income, or someone in a high tax bracket who wants to keep more of earnings. Whatever the case, the goal is to maximize the current income.

Although the income category includes some safe investments, it also provides a higher return. Two products in the income category are municipal and corporate bonds.

Municipal bonds, issued by cities, states, and counties, are federally tax-free. If you buy these bonds within the state where you live, they may also be exempt from state and local taxes.

Corporate bonds can give you good returns if taxes are not a major concern.

Growth Investments

Increasing your wealth through the growth of your investment dollars should be one of your top priorities. Too many investors have confused investing with speculating, which is just plain gambling. Careful planning and selection can help you minimize risk as you achieve your financial goals.

Investing for growth means accepting a low current yield in return for watching your investment grow in value over the years. Common stocks and real estate are excellent investments for growth.

Other investors have chosen to invest in stocks and real estate through mutual funds. Stock funds have averaged 12 percent a year over the last fifteen years. That means your money would double about every five to six years.

You can invest in real estate through a limited partnership, sometimes with as little as $1,000.

HIGH-YIELD INVESTMENTS

The year 1987 was supposed to be a bonanza for investors looking for income investments. With tax reform, the maximum tax rate dropped from 50 percent to 33 percent in 1987, allowing investors to keep more of the income they earned.

The outlook for fixed-income investments seemed bright; yields on the thirty-year treasury bond dropped from near 14 percent in 1984 to 7.50 percent. Bondholders enjoyed sizable capital gains and income that stayed well above the inflation rate.

Investors were shocked in March and April of 1987 as interest rates started to head upward while bond prices dropped. Bondholders and shareholders in fixed-income mutual funds lost as much as 10 percent of their principal. Still, that has not dampened the appeal of high-yield investments. They include income-producing products that offer above-average returns, higher than money market funds and CDs.

Investors continue to scramble for products like municipal

bonds, real estate limited partnerships, mortgage-backed securities, and junk bonds.

High-Yield Bonds: One Way to Earn Above-Average Returns

High-yield bonds, or junk bonds as they are better known, are debt obligations of troubled companies and bonds issued to finance takeovers and other corporate reorganizations. These so-called junk bonds pay as much as 2 to 4 percent more than blue-chip bonds. Junk bonds represent low-rated, often unsecured debt. The 4 percent higher yield differential is supposed to compensate investors for the additional risk.

As with all bonds, the risks are twofold. The first is market risk. When interest rates go up, all bonds eventually decline in price. The second is credit risk. Will you get your money back? Since World War II, the average default rate for all corporate bonds has been around 1 percent. For low-grade bonds, the default rate has been about 1.5 percent.

The best and safest way to invest in junk bonds is through a high-yield bond mutual fund. In a mutual fund, the portfolio is diversified with twenty or more industries. If one company should default, the effect on the portfolio won't be disastrous.

Choosing a High-Yield Bond Fund

In most successful high-yield bond funds, any one issue is not more than 2 percent of the total portfolio. Select a fund that can invest in safer investments, such as government securities, when the market changes.

Look for a family of mutual funds that has a good research department because investing in junk bonds requires research similar to that involved when investing in stocks.

Also, check the average maturity of the bonds in the portfolio. The longer the term of the bond, the greater its exposure to risk. Bonds with maturities of seven to ten years will not fluctuate as much as bonds with twenty- to thirty-year maturities. Finally, make sure you read the prospectus and all the sales literature carefully.

Investing in Real Estate for High Yields

A real estate limited partnership is one investment that yields high income. As a limited partner, you can own a share in a pool of properties or mortgages without being liable for anything more than your initial investment.

Limited partnerships buy income-producing properties or make mortgage loans and pass the income and tax benefits on to the limited partners.

The benefits of a limited partnership are offset by its being difficult to sell in a hurry. You should purchase one only if you plan to hold the investment for at least seven to ten years. The tax laws are making highly leveraged partnerships less attractive. Most partnerships will provide high income and a share of property appreciation.

They have yielded as much as 7 to 13 percent and can be bought for a minimum of $5,000. Generally, the deals are structured to provide some tax benefits with 20 to 100 percent of the income sheltered.

High Income with Municipal Bonds

It's not what you earn that's important; it's what you get to keep. In this case, municipal bonds may be just what you need. Historically, the interest on bonds issued by state and local governments and certain related institutions has been exempt from federal taxes.

Income from these bonds is usually exempt from state and local taxes if you live in the state of the issuer. Analysts recommend sticking with high-quality issues rated A or better.

Bonds typically have a face value of $1,000 and are sold in lots of five. If you don't have $20,000 or more to invest, you would probably be wise to invest in a municipal bond mutual fund. They have generally lower minimums and can pay as high as 8 percent, and in addition, they are exempt from federal taxes. For someone in the 28 percent tax bracket, that would be equivalent to a taxable bond paying 11 percent.

HOW TO INVEST $1,000

Whether you are starting an investment portfolio from scratch or building on a tower of assets, you will most likely build it in increments of $1,000. Investing $1,000 at a time makes sense for at least two reasons. First, most investments require at least $1,000. Second, $1,000 is small enough to put in one investment.

Where do you put your $1,000? Well, that depends on your financial objectives, your net worth, the amount of risks you want to take, and the other investments already in your portfolio.

If you will need the money in a couple of years, you don't want to risk losing it. The larger your portfolio and the longer the term of the investment, the more risks you can be willing to take.

Double Your Money in Ten Years!: Low-Risk Investing

Among the safest places to invest $1,000 are money market accounts offered by banks and money market mutual funds. Your choices can be narrowed even further by selecting taxable or tax-free money market vehicles.

Your money will earn a high yield in a short-term certificate of deposit (CD) and even more in a long-term CD than it would in a money market account or fund. If you lock up your money in a longer-term CD, you may miss out on higher yields later on. Other selections include short-term bond funds. Make sure you select a fund with bonds maturing in three years or less.

For a minimum of $25, you can invest in Series EE U.S. savings bonds. The interest is exempt from state and local income tax, and federal taxes are deferred until you redeem the bond.

Double Your Money in Seven Years!

If you are willing to risk losing some of your money in hopes of a better payoff, you may want to select investments that have a moderate amount of risk. Total return funds allow you to be cushioned against stock and bond losses by being diversified.

Balanced funds invest in stocks and bonds. They get their growth from stocks and the income from bonds. They can change their investment mix to adjust to the current economic environment.

Growth and income funds, on the other hand, invest mainly in conservative stocks that pay good dividends. Of course, some funds invest in undervalued, out-of-favor stocks that hold up well in a bad stock market. For income-oriented investors, there are Ginnie Mae (Government National Mortgage Association) funds.

Double Your Money in Four Years!

When you're investing for high return, expect high risk. You must remember to never invest in anything you don't understand and never invest more than you can afford to lose. A rise in the stock market does wonders for large blue-chip stocks. But an opportunity may be available in stocks of smaller companies, those with outstanding shares worth $100 million or less.

Since small company stocks generally trade for $10 or less, you can pick up one hundred shares with a $1,000 investment. Consider these low-priced stocks only for a well-diversified portfolio.

Gold, with wide fluctuations in price, should be a part of any diversified portfolio. At a price of around $450 an ounce, you can pick up two one-ounce gold coins or buy shares in a gold mutual fund that invests in gold mining companies.

INVESTMENT CLUBS

Thinking about investing but don't have a lot of money? An investment club will give you diversification and an educational experience. The clubs work like a mutual fund, with one distinction. You and your fellow investors call the shots.

In an investment club, members pool their money and pick investments as a team. The average club has fifteen members and each member puts in about $30 per month, according to the National Association of Investors Corporation (NAIC).

Today 6,500 clubs with more than 100,000 members are part of the NAIC, a national nonprofit organization that helps member clubs organize and invest. The organization maintains that the average club earns 20 percent on its portfolio.

Why Start an Investment Club?

There are several benefits to starting an investment club. If you can get fifteen to twenty people working together in a club, you have funds available to diversify to a much greater extent than any member could on an individual basis.

Sharing research is another advantage to being in an investment club. With each member spending an hour or two per week researching investments, a lot of analysis can be produced. Each member gains from the overall research efforts of the group.

Involvement is critical to the success of the club. If two or three people end up doing all the work, a club is not likely to last long. Sharing the duties improves the benefits and profits for everyone in the club.

The experience that members gain aids in managing personal investments while adding profits to the club's portfolio.

Organizing Your Club

Every month, 125 new investment clubs form and join the NAIC. After eighteen months, nearly half of the new clubs are still operating. Setting up an investment club is not difficult as long as you follow some simple guidelines.

First, select members from people with whom you have something in common. Schedule a meeting and ask friends and associates to invite their friends. Expect 40 percent to either decline joining or lose interest after several months.

Consider the personalities of the potential members. You should enjoy each other's company. If all goes well, you will be meeting as a group every month and investing together for many years.

Setting Investment Goals

When you're setting up an investment club, one of the first things you will do is determine how much each member will contribute every month. The amount can vary from as little as $10 to $100 or more.

A newly formed club should start out with each member contributing the same amount each month. This standard simplifies record keeping and reporting. Members should see their investment as a long-term venture and shouldn't expect to realize any profits for the first two or three years.

Next, the members should document the club's investment goals in writing.

Final Guidelines

Most investment clubs organize as partnerships with annual profits assigned to members on a per-share basis. This approach is the most manageable one for a club.

You have to anticipate that some people may want to give up their membership. To pay off departing members without disrupting the club's portfolio, invest a portion of the total portfolio in a liquid account—for example, a money market fund.

One of the most crucial guidelines to follow when organizing an investment club is the assignment of responsibilities. It would be wise to include a bookkeeper as a member to assure that accurate records are kept. Every member should spend equal time researching investments and taking care of other club business.

An investment club can provide you with a rich opportunity to earn a good return on your money while offering an educational experience as well. For more information, write the National Association of Investors Corporation, 1515 East Eleven Mile Road, Royal Oak, Michigan 48067, or call 313-543-0612.

HOW TO EARN 10 PERCENT ON YOUR MONEY

High-yield earnings are not as hard to get as you may think. With rates fluctuating, now may be a time to lock in a good yield.

When rates are moving lower, income investments can provide total returns that come close to those of growth investments. An option to consider is a municipal bond mutual fund. This kind of fund invests in bonds issued by states, cities, and county governments.

The interest is federally tax-free, and some of the dividends may be exempt from state tax if the fund invests in bonds in your state. Yields of 6 to 7 percent tax-free are available. If you are married and earn more than $31,000 a year, or you are single and earn more than $18,500, you are in the 28 percent tax bracket. In this example, a 7 percent yield is equivalent to 10 percent or more on a taxable investment.

Earn 10 Percent with Corporate Bonds

Tired of investing in the same old thing? Out for some excitement and a higher yield, too? Corporate bonds could be the answer.

Investing for high yields involves taking a certain amount of risk, and buying shares in a corporate bond fund is not for everyone. But if you have diversified your money and want to earn high yields, corporate bond funds deserve a closer look. Corporate bond mutual funds invest in bonds of companies such as Turner Broadcasting, MGM/United Artists, Home Shopping Network, and the Fruit of the Loom Company. Bonds of these companies carry higher interest rates but offer more risk in that they may default (not make their interest payments).

Yields on corporate bond funds can be as high as 14 percent. As an investor, you have to decide whether the higher yield compensates you for the additional risk you are taking. Make that decision after you have read the fund's prospectus and other material carefully.

DIAMONDS AS AN INVESTMENT

Diamonds have long been a representation of wealth and power. Valued by manufacturers for their hardness, nearly 60 percent of the world's diamonds are used for items like drill bits. Most of the world's diamonds come from Africa and the Commonwealth of Independent States (formerly the Soviet Union).

Diamonds are distributed to the market by DeBeers Consolidated Mines Ltd., a cartel that has controlled the market since 1900. Eight out of every ten diamonds on the market are controlled by the cartel.

Speculative investing in diamonds should be reserved for the more sophisticated investor. But if you're looking to purchase a diamond for an engagement ring, anniversary gift, or other purpose, be sure to buy one with good investment qualities. Four factors determine the value of a diamond—color, clarity, cut, and carat.

How Color Affects the Value of Diamonds

Diamond dealers expect the value of diamonds to at least keep pace with inflation. When selecting a diamond, remember that color is the most important factor in determining its value. The diamond's color cannot be determined by the untrained eye. Most diamonds, fashioned as jewelry, contain a minute trace of yellow, brown, or gray. The most rare and expensive diamonds are colorless or white.

The color grade given a perfectly clear stone is D Color. A diamond graded as E Color would be next on the scale and is also high in quality but not as clear. Diamonds come in a full range of colors, including red, pink, blue, and yellow.

Can a Diamond Have Imperfections and Still Be Flawless?

When purchasing a diamond, you also want to know about the clarity of the stone. That will affect the price you pay. Clarity refers to the presence of any flaws in the diamond, flaws determined by experts.

A number system is used to grade the diamonds on a scale from flawless to imperfect. A flawless diamond may still contain some modest irregularities that don't materially affect the clarity of the stone. To get a diamond of investment grade quality, purchase one that is as close to flawless as your pocketbook will allow.

The Right Cut

The brilliance and durability of diamonds have always been fascinating. However, in the past few decades, the beauty of diamonds has become a secondary consideration because they are being viewed in terms of their investment potential.

How a diamond is cut will affect its value; a perfect cut brings out the maximum brilliance in a diamond. Eighty percent of the light entering a diamond is absorbed before being refracted. This creates the diamond's legendary "fire."

A perfectly cut diamond maximizes the amount of light returned to the viewer. The more finely proportioned a stone, the higher the value. Popular cuts include the round, the marquise, the oval, the pear, and the emerald.

Selecting the Proper Weight

The physical weight of a diamond is measured in *carats*, not to be confused with the *karat* used to describe the fineness of gold. One carat is equal to .2 gram. In determining the carat weight, laboratories measure the diamonds using extremely accurate electronic scales. The larger carat diamonds have greater investment value because they are rarer.

Many dealers recommend purchase of diamonds in the one- to three-carat weight category. Diamonds over three carats are very hard to sell.

Every investment grade diamond should have a written certification describing the four valuation criteria: color, clarity, cut, and carat. The Gemological Institute of America describes and certifies diamonds for a fee.

INVESTMENT GIFT IDEAS FOR CHILDREN

Whenever the holiday season approaches, your thoughts probably turn to gift ideas for your children, grandchildren, nieces, nephews, brothers, and/or sisters. Along with the latest toys, dolls, and games, another gift option you should consider is a financial investment.

Financial products, just like toys or clothing, come in all shapes and sizes. With a little bit of shopping around, you can find one that matches your budget and also meets the needs of the recipient—whether the gift be college tuition in fifteen years or money for summer camp in three years.

An investment gift can bring both pleasure and comfort to the giver. The specter of college tuition, for example, strikes fear in the hearts of many parents. According to experts, the cost of a four-year college education today averages roughly $17,000 at a public institution and $45,000 at a private institution. So, for children born this year, the cost may reach well into six figures at some schools.

Although a forecast like that can put a damper on holiday spirits, there is a bright side. Through careful planning, you can begin to offset these kinds of expenses today. By giving relatively small amounts to children while they are young, you can salt away enough to take the sting out of the college years looming ahead.

The key is giving money to children early and using appropriate investment vehicles. During their growing-up years, the dividends and interest from their investments will compound at their low tax rate or will be completely tax-free. However, to qualify for the tax advantage, the money must ultimately be used for acceptable purposes such as school tuition, ballet lessons, or summer camp, and not for the child's everyday living expenses. Check your state's laws to find out exactly how this money may be used.

Each child may receive as much as $10,000 per year from an individual, or $20,000 from a couple, without having to pay federal gift tax. But a tax-free investment of just $4,000 at 10 percent interest today will blossom into more than $16,500 at the end of fifteen years.

How Should You Give Money to Children?

Building a financial nest egg for children can be easily done by establishing a custodial account, or a trust, under the Uniform Gifts to Minors Act (UGMA). You can work with an investment professional to open this type of account. You will need a Social Security number for the child and someone to serve as legal custodian for the account. If you are the custodian, the value of the account could be considered part of your estate for tax purposes in the event of your death.

When you set up a trust for a child under the UGMA, the principal and earnings are given to the child permanently. So, be sure you are willing to make a gift that you cannot reclaim at some point later. The IRS carefully scrutinizes UGMA accounts that exceed $30,000. The new tax law places some restrictions on custodial accounts, so consult your tax or legal advisor before you proceed.

You can use a variety of investment products to fund a child's account, for example, zero coupon bonds.

Zero Coupon Bonds

Zero coupon bonds provide one good method for funding a college education. These bonds can be purchased today at a fraction of the value they will have at their maturity. If, for example, you purchase $10,000 in zero coupon bonds that are due to mature in ten years, you would pay only about $3,000 for them.

By allowing you to select an issue that will mature at a date when you will need the money, these bonds offer a convenient way to plan for future expenses such as college tuition.

These bonds do not pay yearly interest; rather, they pay interest when they mature. However, the interest may be taxable at the child's rate as it accrues every year. One option among zero coupon bonds is the municipal tax-free bond, which is exempt from federal tax.

Mutual Funds

Another investment gift idea is mutual fund shares. They offer several advantages: professional management by experts, safety through a diverse portfolio, and liquidity (easy access to your money).

Not all mutual funds are alike. They offer varying degrees of risk and potential for appreciation. Your investment representative can help you choose a fund that best suits your individual needs. Most mutual fund investment companies have a family of funds; you can switch from one kind of fund to another as your investment goals change.

Aggressive growth funds are at the high-risk end of the mutual fund spectrum. Emerging growth stocks offer shareholders good potential for capital gains. For building college money, an aggressive growth fund would probably provide the best return over the years. These funds are designed to generate high long-term earnings and have, in many cases, performed better than the stock market in recent years. The minimum investment required by these funds is usually $1,000.

Money market funds provide a more conservative option, offering high current income while preserving capital. Money market funds invest in short-term debt instruments, and their value goes up as stocks go down. That is a good reason to have the option of shifting your money within a family of funds as the market changes. Money market funds usually require a $1,000 minimum investment. However, they do not require any fees, and shares can be redeemed at any time.

Stocks

One way to get youngsters' attention is to purchase an investment gift that will have significance. Buying stock in a company such as Walt Disney or Toys R Us that makes a popular toy they like or manufactures clothing they wear can be fun. And the gift need not be expensive. You can purchase a couple of shares of stock in a company, and then if the company has a dividend reinvestment plan, you can have the stock dividends automatically reinvested in additional shares. Some companies will also accept additional cash payments from a shareholder to purchase more stock, usually without brokerage fees.

If the recipients of your investment gift are old enough to follow daily market activity in the newspaper, you can provide them with a unique educational experience as well as a sound investment.

INFLATION

Inflation! There are several types, and some may even help your investment program. The U.S. Department of Commerce has reported that the average annual rate of inflation in the United States, as measured by the consumer price index, was about 3 percent between 1950 and 1970.

Between 1970 and 1980, the average annual inflation rate was 7.8 percent. During the late 1970s, the appearance of 9 to 12 percent rates of inflation worried many investors. In the 1980s, inflation was as high as 14 percent and as low as 2 percent. Over the last several years, inflation has stayed at around 3 percent.

Inflation is the economic condition that occurs when the supply of money is out of balance with the supply of things to buy with it. In other words, inflation is too much money chasing too few goods.

That imbalance leads to a sustained increase in prices. Although inflation is not desirable, it can usually be managed. With inflation, you experience an increase in living costs, which puts a squeeze on your budget.

There are at least three types of inflation—cost-push, demand-pull, and printing-press inflation.

Types of Inflation

Cost-push inflation results when an economic force increases the cost of producing goods and services during a specified period, which "pushes up" prices. The force may be external, such as an oil embargo, or production-generated, as with a manufacturer whose production costs increase.

Demand-pull inflation is just the opposite. The demand for goods and services exceeds the available supply. The increased demand "pulls up" prices, resulting in inflation. An example would be the growing number of affluent two-career couples who are searching for housing. This demand may drive up the cost of suburban housing in an area.

Many economists argue that the distinction between cost-push and demand-pull inflation is unimportant. Neither can create a sustained increase in prices unless the Federal Reserve provides an ever-increasing supply of money to accommodate inflation. The Federal Reserve can print more money, creating what is called *printing-press inflation*. With more money chasing a dwindling supply of goods, prices start to rise, and the inflation rate increases.

Printing-press inflation is one of three ways that the government can raise income. The other two ways are imposing taxes and borrowing. Raising taxes is politically unpopular and is used as a last resort. The government can ask people to lend it money by issuing bonds. The U.S. Treasury will sell government debt in the form of treasury bills, notes, and bonds to investors. The result of this action is anti-inflationary.

Inflation and the Consumer Price Index

Can the consumer price index accurately predict your personal rate of inflation? Inflation is measured as an increase in prices, which is calculated by an index that serves as a representation of the rate of inflation.

The most common index used is the consumer price index. When this index rises or falls, it means that the goods or services measured in the index increased or decreased.

Statements about the consumer price index may be meaningless, however, as they apply to your personal situation. If the index includes the price of a steak and a new house, the index accurately reflects your rate of inflation if you eat meat and buy a new house every month. If you don't buy these items every month, the index does not accurately represent your personal rate of inflation. Your life-style gives you a personal inflation rate that may be more or less than the consumer price index.

Misconceptions About Inflation

The rate of inflation affects all of us, but there are many misconceptions about inflation.

You have no doubt heard statements like this one: "At the present rate of inflation, a loaf of bread will cost $10 by the time you retire." Several things are wrong with this statement.

First, there has never been a constant rate of inflation in the United States. At times, the rate of inflation has been as high as 13 percent and as low as 1 percent.

Second, salary increases are often tied to an inflation index, which at least helps your salary keep pace with inflation. The next time someone tells you a loaf of bread will cost $10 at a certain date under a given rate of inflation, apply the same growth rate to your salary.

Third, you don't have to buy a loaf of bread at any price. You're free to substitute one item for another, and this substitution can reduce your exposure to inflation.

SMART MONEY MOVES

You can make some smart money moves to save lots of money. If you keep a sizable amount of money in your checking account, it is probably earning interest at a low rate. Even worse, it might not be earning interest at all.

If you haven't started a savings plan this year, give it a fresh look. Saving $25 a week, invested at 8 percent in a money market account, will grow to more than $1,300 in one year and more than $7,600 in five. One of the most painless ways to save is through payroll deduction.

If you live from paycheck to paycheck, as most people do, now would be a good time to get a grip on your spending habits. Use a home budget book sold by most office supply stores to start keeping tabs on where your money goes. Record every expense for a couple of months. Spending patterns will surface, and you will be able to start planning ways to save money in certain areas. With this "extra" cash, you will be able to lock in high yields.

Your Credit Cards

Paying off your VISA, MasterCard, and department store credit cards will save you money. If you think you can't live without your credit cards, think about this. If you carry a balance of $1,500 on your credit cards, you are probably paying at least 18 percent interest. The finance charges alone will add more than $20 to your bill, even if you don't charge anything for the month.

If you can't erase those debts quickly, shop around for a card with a lower interest rate. Even better, if you own a home, get a home equity loan and pay off your bills. Interest on a home equity loan is fully deductible.

SHOP YOUR INSURANCE

Shopping your insurance coverages may be one of the smartest moves you can make. Call your auto, homeowner's, and life insurance agents and ask for a better price. You may lower your cost if you place all your insurance with one agent.

Increasing the amount of your deductible will save money on auto and homeowner's insurance. In addition, combining more than one car on a policy will surely cut your premium cost.

When buying life insurance, be sure you determine how much you need, then buy all you need. What does that mean? Once you and your insurance agent have determined that you need $100,000 worth of life insurance, be sure you find the least expensive way to buy that much insurance.

After shopping for prices on your insurance coverage, you will almost certainly end up paying a lower premium on at least one policy.

3

YOUR HOME

BUYING VS. RENTING

The decision to buy a home should not be made lightly. Many home buyers have been tempted by books and seminars that promise riches in real estate with "no money down" schemes that promise to make anyone a millionaire.

The reality is that real estate is a solid investment requiring a personal as well as a financial commitment. A down payment is only the beginning. Homeownership involves an ongoing mortgage, tax payments, and expenses such as maintenance and improvements.

Real estate doesn't miraculously appreciate in value. Today, prices are rising about 5 percent a year on the family home. In Houston, the value of homes has dropped as much as 41 percent since 1983 because of falling oil prices. In spite of variations in local prices, buying a home is still a good long-term investment.

When Should You Buy?

Buying a home is a serious investment. If you buy before you are financially able, you could sorely regret your decision. Here are some guidelines to determine if you are ready. Do you have a solid, steady income? Can you afford mortgage payments that may be more than your current rent? Do you plan to stay in your present community for several years? Do you recognize the responsibility involved in buying a home? Can you commit yourself to a down payment and monthly payments on a mortgage loan?

Once you have made the decision to buy, move quickly. Every year you delay, you postpone gaining the tax advantages of homeownership. In addition, you run the risk that the demand for rental property in your area will grow and your rent will increase.

The Advantages of Renting

There are some advantages to renting. Rents have not increased at quite the same rate as the cost of buying a house. Remember, the price of owning a home includes the high cost of maintenance and utilities.

Renters have far less expense for inside and outside upkeep. In an apartment, for instance, your utility costs are lower because supplying heat and light to a complex of ten or twenty units is less expensive per unit than paying for the same utilities in a three-bedroom home.

For city dwellers, renting may be less expensive than buying. With good mass transportation, you don't necessarily have to own a car. And you won't have to deal with constant maintenance and upkeep.

The Disadvantages of Renting

Renting an apartment can have its drawbacks. Rents do go up, sometimes sharply. When was the last time your rent went down after your lease expired? In addition, the building owner may decide to sell to someone else, causing rents to go even higher. Even worse, the owner may convert the units to condos, forcing you to either buy or move out. Home costs, by comparison, may be higher at first but are fixed for the term of your mortgage, as long as thirty years.

When you rent an apartment, you live very close to your neighbors. That can mean less privacy. And noisy and inconsiderate neighbors can make life unbearable.

In making the decision of whether to rent or to buy, take your personal as well as financial considerations into account.

HOW TO BUY A HOUSE

Your rent will be going up the first of the month, and you have had it with the noisy neighbors upstairs, so your thoughts turn to buying a home of your own. What should you consider (see fig. 3.1)?

Typically, not more than 28 percent of your gross income should go toward housing expenses. This amount should include the monthly payment of principal and interest, property taxes, utilities, insurance, and maintenance. If you make $30,000 a year, for example, your total housing expenses each month should not exceed $750. You could afford a $60,000 mortgage at 10 percent with monthly principal and interest payments of approximately $526.

Figure 3.1

HOUSING AFFORDABILITY

Buying a house is a decision that will affect your spending habits, social life, leisure time, and practically every facet of your life. But the financial aspect is the primary concern, especially when you are buying your first house.

THE 36 PERCENT RULE

Most lenders will allow a family to devote up to 36 percent of its gross monthly income to pay for total monthly debt, including home payments, car loans, student loans, credit card billings, and other long-term debt. Of that amount, most lenders will allow 28 percent of gross monthly income to cover principal and interest payments on the mortgage, plus property taxes and home insurance.

FIGURING OUT WHAT YOU CAN AFFORD

The maximum purchase price you can afford will depend on the down payment you are able to make, the interest rate on your loan, and how much money you can afford to spend each month on your home payment. The work sheet below will help you make this calculation.

ESTIMATED MAXIMUM PURCHASE PRICE

1. Cash available for a down payment

Available cash	$________
CDs, stocks, bonds, etc.	+________
Cash gifts	+________
Total cash to be raised	________
Less closing costs	–________
Down payment	$________

2. Gross monthly income

Combined annual income	________
	divided by 12
Gross monthly income	________

3. Affordable monthly PITI

Gross monthly income (from Step 2)	$________
Percent of income allowable for debts	**× 0.36**
Affordable monthly debt	________
Minus actual debt payments other than for housing	–________
Affordable monthly PITI	$________

4. Affordable monthly principal and interest

Affordable monthly PITI (from Step 3)	$________
Minus estimated taxes and insurance	–________
Affordable monthly payment for principal and interest	$________

5. Maximum amount of mortgage loan

Enter the maximum amount from figure 3.2 $__________

6. Maximum purchase price

Enter down payment from Step 1 $__________

Add maximum mortgage loan from Step 5 +__________

Estimated maximum purchase price $__________

FILLING OUT THE SIX-STEP WORK SHEET

1. Cash available for a down payment. Add up the cash you have available to spend on a house; the value of any stocks, certificates of deposit, or other investments you can cash in to buy a house; and any gifts you can get from parents or relatives. This is your total cash to be raised. Estimate your closing costs at 5 percent of the amount of your mortgage; since you don't know exactly what this will be yet, you will have to approximate. Subtract the closing costs from your cash to be raised; the difference is what you can spend on a down payment.

2. Gross monthly income. Get your total annual income from your most recent income tax form; make adjustments if you have received pay raises since then, or if the figure includes income from sources such as sales of stocks. Divide by 12 to get your gross monthly income.

3. Affordable monthly PITI. PITI is short for principal, interest, taxes, and insurance—the components of your monthly home payments. You need to calculate it this way: take your gross monthly income from Step 2 and multiply by .36. From this amount, subtract the amounts you spend on other monthly debt payments, such as for car loans, other loans, and credit card bills. The difference is what you can afford for monthly PITI.

4. Affordable monthly principal and interest. Take the PITI amount you can afford from Step 3, and subtract your estimated monthly payment for taxes and insurance. To determine this number, ask your real estate agent what the approximate costs are for homes in the areas and price ranges in which you are interested. These costs can vary greatly depending on the area. The difference is what you can spend each month on principal and interest.

5. Maximum amount of mortgage loan. Use figure 3.2 to find out how large a mortgage you can afford based on the amount calculated in Step 4. The chart covers interest rates currently available; check with lenders to see which rate you might qualify for.

6. Maximum purchase price. Add the down payment you can afford from Step 1 to the maximum mortgage you can afford from Step 5. The total is the maximum purchase price you can afford.

FIGURE 3.2

MORTGAGE PAYMENT CALCULATOR BASED ON 30-YEAR MORTGAGE

TO USE, SEE FIGURE 3.1.

1. Choose the column for the interest rate for which you can qualify.
2. Look for the amount you can spend each month on principal and interest.
3. The amount at the left of that row is the mortgage amount you can get for that monthly payment. Enter this number in Step 5.

	7.0%	7.5%	8.0%	8.5%
$ 50,000	$ 332.65	$ 349.61	$ 366.88	$ 384.46
$ 60,000	$ 399.18	$ 419.53	$ 440.26	$ 461.35
$ 70,000	$ 465.71	$ 489.45	$ 513.64	$ 538.24
$ 80,000	$ 532.24	$ 559.37	$ 587.01	$ 615.13
$ 90,000	$ 598.77	$ 629.29	$ 660.39	$ 692.02
$100,000	$ 665.30	$ 699.21	$ 733.76	$ 768.91
$110,000	$ 731.83	$ 769.14	$ 807.14	$ 845.80
$120,000	$ 798.36	$ 839.06	$ 880.52	$ 922.70
$130,000	$ 864.89	$ 908.98	$ 953.89	$ 999.59
$140,000	$ 931.42	$ 978.90	$1,027.27	$1,076.48
$150,000	$ 997.95	$1,048.82	$1,100.65	$1,153.37
$160,000	$1,064.48	$1,118.74	$1,174.02	$1,230.26
$170,000	$1,131.01	$1,188.66	$1,247.40	$1,307.15
$180,000	$1,197.54	$1,258.59	$1,320.78	$1,384.04
$190,000	$1,264.07	$1,328.51	$1,394.15	$1,460.94
$200,000	$1,330.60	$1,398.43	$1,467.53	$1,537.83

	9.0%	9.5%	10.0%
$ 50,000	$ 402.31	$ 420.43	$ 438.79
$ 60,000	$ 482.77	$ 504.51	$ 526.54
$ 70,000	$ 563.24	$ 588.60	$ 614.30
$ 80,000	$ 643.70	$ 672.68	$ 702.06
$ 90,000	$ 724.16	$ 756.77	$ 789.81
$100,000	$ 804.62	$ 840.85	$ 877.57
$110,000	$ 885.08	$ 924.94	$ 965.33
$120,000	$ 965.55	$1,009.03	$1,053.09
$130,000	$1,046.01	$1,093.11	$1,140.84
$140,000	$1,126.47	$1,177.20	$1,228.60

	9.0%	9.5%	10.0%
$150,000	$1,206.93	$1,261.28	$1,316.36
$160,000	$1,287.40	$1,345.37	$1,404.11
$170,000	$1,367.86	$1,429.45	$1,491.87
$180,000	$1,448.32	$1,513.54	$1,579.63
$190,000	$1,528.78	$1,597.62	$1,667.39
$200,000	$1,609.25	$1,681.71	$1,755.14

Finding a Real Estate Agent

Armed with the knowledge of current financing rates and the price range you can afford to pay, you will want to find the "right" real estate agent to help you locate your dream home.

A real estate agent is a person licensed and authorized to buy and sell property for others. Finding the right agent means checking around and asking friends for referrals. A good professional should be able to satisfy both the seller and the buyer. But never forget, the agent works for the seller.

Tell the agent exactly what you are looking for—the price, size, location, and conveniences. Some questions to keep in mind when dealing with a real estate agent are these: Were you shown houses in your price range? Does the agent really understand what you are looking for?

Selecting the Right Neighborhood

When buying a house, you are also shopping for a community and a neighborhood. You will want to make inquiries regarding property taxes, schools, shopping areas, and so on.

Tax on a house is a continuing expense. It is, however, deductible from your federal tax return, just as your mortgage interest payments are. Property taxes vary but tend to be higher the closer you live to a big city.

Check the quality of local schools by talking with parents

of children who are already enrolled or by visiting with teachers and PTA members.

Another factor to consider is the convenience of the shopping areas, churches, parks, and other recreation facilities. Also, consider how far you will have to commute to work. In evaluating these factors, look for a neighborhood that is stabilized or, even better, still improving.

Negotiating the Best Price

Most listed real estate is sold within 5 percent of the asking price. Never offer to pay the asking price until you have surveyed the market and feel secure that the price is fair.

Once a price is agreed upon, a sales contract is prepared. It is a standard form used by Realtors and attorneys to which clauses or conditions may be added. The contract will include your offering price and all the conditions involved in the purchase.

For example, almost every offer includes the condition that financing will be approved. Other conditions may include the completion of repairs needed, as determined by termite or home inspection reports, and the successful sale of your present home. Negotiating can ensure that you buy the house you want at a fair price.

Financing Your Dream Home

Shopping for a mortgage is just as important as selecting the right house. There are basically two sources for mortgages: government and conventional loans. The most popular government loans are FHA and VA.

The Federal Housing Administration (FHA) is an agency of the Department of Housing and Urban Development (HUD). FHA loans are insured by HUD. The loans are meant to help low- and moderate-income people buy homes. To qualify, you must meet certain income and credit criteria. The property you want to buy must meet FHA requirements. A major advantage of getting an FHA loan is the low down payment, usually about 3 percent of the purchase price versus 10 to 20 percent for conventional loans. Ask your lender how you can apply for one.

The Veterans Administration (VA) guarantees low or no down payment loans for the purchase of a home if you are a veteran or the spouse of a veteran. Check with your local VA office to see if you qualify.

Conventional loans are supplied by banks, savings and loans, and insurance and mortgage companies. Before you commit to a loan, you will want to know the interest rate, the number of years the mortgage spans, how much your down payment will be, and what will be included in the closing costs.

Most mortgages are either fixed-rate or adjustable-rate mortgages (better known as ARMs). The type of mortgage you get will be determined by the monthly payment you can afford. Adjustable-rate mortgages usually have a lower initial interest rate than fixed-rate mortgages, which could allow you to qualify for a larger loan and a more expensive home.

Fifteen-Year Mortgages

Consumer interest in fifteen-year mortgages has surged. It is easy to see why. First, rates are lower on the fifteen-year mortgage as compared to the traditional thirty-year loan, generally at least .5 percentage point or less.

Second, a fifteen-year loan will be paid off in half the time of a thirty-year loan. You will save 50 to 60 percent in interest charges over the term of the loan.

Third, the monthly interest and principal payment will be higher on a fifteen-year loan, but your equity in your home will build faster than with a thirty-year loan.

Before you agree to a thirty-year mortgage loan, investigate a shorter term loan. It may help cut interest costs and build equity faster.

The Buy-Now-and-Pay-Later Mortgage

The graduated-payment mortgage is back. It is a mortgage loan that begins with a low monthly payment that rises by a specific amount over a period of time. The interest rate on a GPM, as it is called, might start out as low as 6 percent.

The initial installment on a $100,000 GPM would be only $830 compared with $1,100 on a fixed-rate mortgage. This difference may allow you to qualify for a loan that may have been out of reach before. Lenders can approve borrowers for GPMs based on their ability to afford the low first-year payments.

Before you sign up, though, you should be confident your income will increase enough to keep up with payment increases. A graduated-payment mortgage may allow you to afford a house now and let your income catch up with the increased payments. But as with any loan, be sure to read all the fine print in the application form.

Your Mortgage Loan and Points

Often, home buyers don't realize the effect of points on their mortgage loans. Points, which are paid in cash at closing, are added to keep the mortgage rate down.

Points increase the yield on the mortgage for the lender and help cover loan closing costs. Each point equals 1 percent of the loan amount. If you get a mortgage for $60,000, one point means you pay $600 to the lender.

The number of points varies depending on the type of loan. Lenders often have a menu of rates and will charge one, two, or three points. Home buyers are not usually sensitive to points because they don't fully understand how they affect their overall costs. A key factor to determining what combination of interest rate and points is right for you is to consider how long you plan to stay in the house.

Mortgage Points and Your Mortgage Rate

The number of points you pay on your home loan will add to your effective annual rate. Which is cheaper: a home mortgage at 8.5 percent interest with three points, or a 9 percent loan with one point? Answer: the 9 percent loan, but only for the first few years.

If you plan to stay in your house twenty years or so, the points don't matter. The shorter the time you plan to keep the house, the more points add to the effective annual rate. That's why a 9 percent loan with one point can be cheaper than the 8.5 percent loan with three points.

Points for home purchase mortgages are tax-deductible for the year in which they are paid. Keep in mind that points are negotiable. Home sellers eager to dispose of their property may agree to split points with the buyer.

REFINANCE YOUR MORTGAGE

With mortgage rates in the single digits, now may be a good time to refinance your home mortgage if your current interest rate is high. You may also be wise to refinance and pay off a second mortgage or a home equity loan.

As a general rule of thumb, you will want to refinance only if you plan to stay in the house at least three more years and if rates have fallen two percentage points from what you are paying now. It will take between two and three years to recoup the refinancing costs, which generally will total 3 to 4 percent of the total loan.

To get the best deal on refinancing, check first with your current mortgage lender because the lender may have some streamlined programs that will save you money. If that doesn't work, shop around and compare rates and fees. And consider refinancing to a fifteen-year mortgage to take advantage of the benefits discussed earlier.

REVERSE MORTGAGES

Still trying to figure out how you will retire? As the average age of the American population increases, many older people don't have enough money to retire comfortably, or they are outliving their retirement income.

To alleviate this problem, many financial institutions are offering retirees with homes a way to supplement their income. It's called the reverse annuity mortgage, and here's how it works. A homeowner takes out a loan against the house, and instead of sending checks to the mortgage company, the lender sends monthly checks to the homeowner. The loan is not repaid until the homeowner sells, leases, or refinances the home, or the homeowner dies.

This mortgage program is generally available only to older people. It allows retirees to retain homeownership while providing needed cash. But a reverse annuity mortgage is not for everyone. There are some alternatives.

One would be for the family to purchase the home from the homeowner and allow him or her to live in it. Banding together with other relatives to complete the purchase will make it easier not only to qualify but to afford the monthly mortgage payments. You will also qualify for tax benefits, and when the retiree dies, you can either rent the house or sell it.

For more information on the reverse mortgage or the alternative, contact your local banker.

LEASE-PURCHASE ON THE RISE

Trying to buy a home but don't have the cash? Many families are embracing lease-purchase arrangements to buy a home. Under this arrangement, would-be home buyers rent a house until they can accumulate enough money for a down payment. The agreements generally run from one to two years. The seller of the home may credit part of the rental payments toward the purchase price.

In addition to first-time home buyers using this arrangement, many buyers moving from other cities are leasing a home for a while until they can get the equity out of the other home.

Some tips before entering a lease-purchase. Try to set the sale price in advance, and make sure you know what percentage of the rental payments is going toward the down payment. Also, you would be wise to get a real estate attorney to review the documents.

WHEN YOUR MORTGAGE IS SOLD

There is a good chance that your home mortgage will be sold to another lender during the life of the loan. Getting a request for a mortgage payment from a lender you've never heard of may come as a shock to you. But hold on; help is on the way. Recently, the Federal National Mortgage Association, nicknamed Fannie Mae, adopted new rules that require the lender to

- give you notice that the mortgage is being sold.
- tell who the buyer is.
- tell how to contact the buyer.

In addition, the company must notify you fifteen days before the next payment is due.

Your former mortgage company must send you the date of the loan transfer and the date of your first payment to the new mortgage holder. Your former lender is also required to send you a confirmation of the switchover, along with other detailed information about payment procedures.

HOMEOWNER'S INSURANCE

Although Americans spend $80 billion each year for property and liability insurance, many don't know what they are receiving for their money, and most are unaware of the gaps that exist in their coverage in the form of overinsurance and underinsurance.

Homeowner's insurance covers your real and personal property against loss. In addition, it protects you against personal liability, medical payments, and property damage caused by persons other than you, the insured.

The term *homeowner's insurance* is misleading. Standard packages cover almost everything you own, plus credit card losses, medical bills, and even personal liability. For example, if one of your credit cards is stolen, your name forged, and purchases made without your knowledge, your insurance company will typically pay up to $1,000 toward your losses.

Understanding Your Policy

Homeowner's insurance is often thought of as a single type of insurance policy. Four different forms are available for homeowners, and two other forms for renters and condominium owners.

Policies are divided into two sections. Section one deals with property protection and covers your home and its contents. The amount of coverage is based on the cost of replacing the entire house. Your personal property is usually covered up to a limit of 50 percent of the cost of your home.

Section two deals with liability protection. It guards you against personal liability, medical payments to others, and damage to other people's property. The range of coverage under a standard policy can be enormous. However, you are covered only for losses named in the policy unless you have all-risk coverage, as in a policy that is type H0-3 (see fig. 3.3 for explanation).

How Much Insurance Do You Need?

Selecting the right amount of homeowner's insurance means looking in the right place. Focus your attention on section one in your policy. Be sure to indicate that the contents of your house are to be insured for "replacement cost." Then if there is a loss, you are given money to actually replace, repair, or rebuild your house.

This replacement coverage refers only to the physical structure; coverage on the contents is typically on an actual cash value. Your replacement will be calculated after subtracting the depreciation in the event you suffer a loss.

Insure your personal property for every dollar value of property you have in your home. If your property is worth $80,000, buy $80,000 worth of insurance for your personal property.

Updating Your Insurance

Review and update your homeowner's insurance every year. The value of your home and possessions fluctuates. Some policies have an "inflation guard" feature that allows the value of your home to keep pace with inflation, but that may not be enough. Reviewing your policy annually will keep your coverage in line with the value of your possessions.

Besides being insured, you must be able to prove what you have. Take a complete inventory, listing and describing every item you own. Note the purchase price and the estimated date you bought it.

If you own video equipment, you can make a personal inventory by videotaping the entire house. Keep a copy of the tape and list outside your home, perhaps in a safe-deposit box. In the event of fire, it would not be destroyed.

Getting the Best Deal

Prices for homeowner's insurance can vary, but there are some ways you can make sure you get the best deal.

Above all, shop around. Compare rates on similar policies (see fig. 3.3). Consider buying all your insurance policies from the same agent or company. You may be able to get a price break if the same insurer writes all your coverage.

Many insurers offer discounts up to 10 percent if you install various safety and security features in your home, such as fire and smoke alarms, deadbolt locks, and fire extinguishers. You can also cut your rates by raising the amount of your deductible, the amount you pay before the insurance takes over.

Although your homeowner's insurance is a necessary part of your insurance coverage, it doesn't have to cost you an arm and a leg.

FIGURE 3.3

HOME INSURANCE

If you own a home, condominium, or cooperative, you need enough of the right kind of insurance to cover it. If you rent, you need insurance to cover your possessions. Use the work sheet below to sort out different types of policies available and determine the coverage you need.

Feature	Recommendation	Policy 1 Coverage	Annual Premium Cost	Policy 2 Coverage	Annual Premium Cost
1. Type: HO-1, HO-2, HO-3, HO-4, HO-5, HO-6	See below, based on your type of home	________	________	________	________
2. Value of home	100% of replacement cost	________	________	________	________
3. Property insurance	Replacement cost	________	________	________	________
4. Liability insurance	$300,000+	________	________	________	________
5. Deductibles	Highest you can afford	________	________	________	________
TOTAL PREMIUM COST			$________		$________

HOW TO FILL OUT THE WORK SHEET

1. Type. Different types of policies exist for house owners, condominium or cooperative owners, and renters.

House policies. House owners have four types of policies from which to choose; all provide limited coverage for personal belongings in the home.

HO-1 policies require that cause of loss be specifically named in your policy. For example, if your furnace explodes and destroys your home, "explosion" must be listed.

HO-2 policies typically cover explosion, fire, storms, theft, vandalism, and the like, but the cause of damage must be listed in the policy.

HO-3 policies are different in that they cover everything except what the policy specifically excludes—usually earthquakes, floods, termites, and rodents.

HO-5 policies offer the same coverage on the building as HO-3 but add more coverage on the contents.

For most people, the benefits of HO-5 are not worth the cost, and they are better off with HO-3.

Condominium or cooperative policies. Condominium owners are covered by HO-6 policies; the coverage includes personal property. Condo owners must make sure their policies cover anything that the condominium association's master policy does not cover. Cooperative owners also benefit from HO-6 policies, even though many of the property coverages do not apply because of the nature of cooperative ownership.

Renter policies. Apartment renters are covered by HO-4 policies, which cover the contents of the apartment.

2. Value of home. You must base your insurance on the replacement cost of your home, not its market value. The market value of your home could be higher than the replacement cost because market value includes your land, which is not covered by insurance; or the market value could be lower than the replacement cost if your home has a lot of handcrafted touches in it. Some insurance companies offer guaranteed replacement. If you insure your home for 100 percent of the value determined by the insurance company, your home would be replaced regardless of the rebuilding cost. If your policy has no such clause, you would receive only up to the amount of the policy.

The 80 percent threshold. If your home is insured for less than 80 percent of replacement cost, most insurance companies also take depreciation into account. For example, if the kitchen in your $100,000 home is destroyed and your home is insured for less than 80 percent of its replacement cost, the insurance company might agree that it costs $20,000 to replace the kitchen, but that your home was so old you should get only $5,000. If your home is insured at 80 percent or more of its replacement cost, you would get a brand-new kitchen. But if your house is destroyed and you are insured for only 80 percent of its replacement cost, you would receive only $80,000.

3. Property insurance. Property insurance covers your dwelling, other structures on your property, personal property including the contents of your home, landscaping, and additional living expenses you might encounter if you have to move out of your home while it is being repaired after an accident. Usually, you select the amount of coverage for your dwelling, and the amounts of the other coverages are a percentage of that. For example, if your dwelling is covered for $100,000, typically your personal property covered would be 50 percent of that, or $50,000. Check with your agent for details; if you need more for personal property or other categories, it can be added.

4. Liability insurance. This amount covers incidents such as somebody slipping and injuring himself on your property or your dog biting somebody. The standard amount is $100,000, but for a small fee, most companies will increase it to $300,000.

5. Deductibles. The highest you can afford is best; $500 is typical, but check with your agent, and be aware that you must pay that amount before insurance coverage begins.

HOME ALARMS

The only free way to protect your home from burglary is to keep your doors and windows locked. For under $100, you can buy extra door locks, mechanical light timers, and motion detectors. Thieves tend to avoid homes where entry looks challenging.

For the best protection, you'll want to consider professionally installed alarms. They come in two styles—wired and wireless—and can cost up to $1,500 and more. For a lot less money, between $300 and $1,000, you can buy a do-it-yourself alarm. Monitoring fees for either professionally or self-installed systems average about $25 a month.

The benefits of protection devices far outweigh the cost consideration because they protect your valuables and qualify you for discounts on your homeowner's insurance. Check with your agent for details.

HOME EQUITY LOANS

Should you hock your home? It's something to consider while bankers are eager to offer you loans that take advantage of recent tax law changes. Interest deductions on most loans have not been available since 1990, but interest on loans secured by a first or second home remains deductible.

Here's how a home equity loan works. The amount of equity in your home is the market value of the house minus whatever you owe on the mortgage. If you could sell your house for $80,000 and you still owe $30,000, your equity is $50,000. Your banker will allow you to use that $50,000 as collateral for a line of credit, an equity loan.

Lenders will not let you borrow the entire amount of equity. They protect themselves with a certain margin of safety in case they have to foreclose on your house and property prices have dropped. However, most banks will allow you to borrow up to 80 percent of your equity.

When Is a Home Equity Loan a Second Mortgage?

Technically, home equity loans are second mortgages. With a second mortgage, a homeowner receives a lump-sum loan, then repays the principal and interest in equal monthly installments over a set time period, similar to car loans. In the case of a home equity loan, you apply for a line of credit much like the one on a credit card. When you need to borrow money, you simply write a check. You are charged interest only on the amount you borrow.

The way you repay equity loans varies from lender to lender. Some require you to pay only interest each month, with principal due at the end. Others ask you to pay something on the principal each month.

Lenders Offer Attractive Interest Rates

While interest rates on unsecured loans are hovering in the mid-teens, and most bank credit card rates are still stuck near 20 percent, home equity loans are as low as 8 percent. One reason for the lower rate is that an equity loan is secured by your house, which reduces the lender's risk. Another reason is that most home equity loans carry variable interest rates, allowing lenders to raise the rate if interest rates go up. Finally, lenders don't have to factor in points when they calculate the annual percentage rate, so the rates appear lower.

A Word of Caution

You should be concerned about some things if you are considering a home equity loan. You may have to pay large closing costs out of proportion to the amount you borrow. Also, there are variable interest rates with no limit on how high the rate can go. Watch out for advertised low initial rates that quickly vanish.

With a home equity loan, you run the risk of losing your house if you don't keep up your payments. Never borrow money without knowing the interest rate.

If you must use your home as collateral for a loan, a fixed-rate second mortgage would be a better choice. If you still choose a home equity loan, know all the facts. Don't grab for the carrot before taking a good look at the stick.

SELLING YOUR HOME

It can be tough selling your home with a recession hanging over the economy.

Selling your house in a "soft" real estate market requires hard work before you put it on the market. You have to make sure the house is attractive to buyers so you can get top dollar. Here are some tips that may make the task a little easier.

List your house with a knowledgeable local broker who will market it aggressively. Make sure the broker plans to advertise your house through a multiple-listing service, which alerts every agent in the area that your house is for sale. Ask the broker about other plans for finding buyers.

Once you have selected a broker, don't argue over the commission; it's the broker's incentive to work hard for you. In fact, you might want to offer a higher commission than the average 6 percent as an incentive to push your home harder.

Setting the Right Price

When you're selling your home, setting a reasonable price is the most important decision you will make. Use recent selling prices of comparable homes in your neighborhood as a guide. You might want to add a 5 to 10 percent negotiating cushion to your asking price, but too high a price could scare away potential buyers.

Make repairs and improvements before you put your house on the market. However, be aware that major remodeling rarely pays off. Concentrate on cosmetic changes to enhance your home's look. A simple improvement such as a new paint job, inside and out, can work wonders. Trim the hedges and keep the grass cut. Perhaps some basic landscaping may be needed. Adding new carpet will give the house a fresh look. Also, repair drooping gutters and any damaged window screens.

If your house still cannot be sold, you might have to consider creative financing.

Creative Financing

When you're trying to sell your house in a slow real estate market, offering financial incentives may help you clinch a sale. Rather than lower the asking price, why not offer a cash rebate of $1,000 to $5,000?

Why a cash rebate instead of a price reduction? A price reduction saves the buyer money on the future mortgage payments but does not help much with immediate expenses.

Most people are really straining their budget to afford the house. With a cash rebate, they receive cash to start decorating or to use toward other needs.

Another way to close a sale is to help the buyer with the costs of a mortgage by offering to pay the buyer's points (the up-front fee charged by the lender).

HOW TO SELL YOUR HOME IN A SLOW MARKET

When trying to sell your home in a slow housing market, you can do some things to help. First, don't be greedy! Setting the price too high can cause the house to stay on the market too long, and that can create a negative image of the property.

Next, get more than one appraisal. Compare them carefully and decide what you can realistically expect to receive, then add about 10 percent to that price. Forget what your neighbor sold his house for last year. It's a different market now. Competition is stiff, and appreciation has slowed.

Be wary of agents who promise to get whatever price you want for the house. Some agents will promise the moon to get you to list the house with them. In some areas, agents who list property get a sales commission no matter who actually sells the house; that's their benefit for getting you to sign a listing contract.

A HOMEOWNER'S ASSOCIATION

A homeowner's association is a nonprofit corporation created by a developer to protect the property and property value in a community. Its primary job is to enforce the association's rules and regulations.

The association controls architectural standards, in other words, the overall look of the community. It can go as far as to dictate what color a home can be painted on the exterior.

The association has the right to file liens on a homeowner's lot, impose late fees, and charge interest on unpaid dues. And yes, it can sue any homeowner for not abiding by the rules.

The association is required to file tax returns and pay taxes like other corporations. It must be covered by liability, property, and other types of insurance.

But most important to you, the homeowner, the association has the power to protect your property from almost anything that could diminish its value, such as poorly maintained lawns or improperly stored vehicles.

Buying into a subdivision can mean automatic membership in the homeowner's association, something you should check out before finalizing purchase of your home. Make sure you read over and agree with the rules and regulations of the association. Know what the assessment fees are, and find out if there are any additional costs to you as a homeowner. For small neighborhoods, these costs can be as little as $50 to $100 a year. In larger neighborhoods, with pools and tennis courts, the monthly assessment may go much higher.

Determine that the association is insured and has been operating successfully. And check that the property looks well-maintained. Remember, the association can, and most often will, enforce its rules, and it can sue you if you do not comply. So, be sure the association meets with your approval as well.

Creating Your Own

You, as a homeowner, can create a homeowner's association in an existing subdivision or neighborhood. First, do all you can to get 100 percent participation from the other homeowners. The association is less successful without total commitment, but you cannot force any homeowner to join a newly created association. Next, establish a governing body and contact a real estate attorney to work out the arrangements.

After your association is up and running, operate it professionally because it can be sued for injuries incurred on the property, for not enforcing the rules, or for enforcing them in a discriminatory manner.

Your association may seem to benefit you only socially at first, but it can increase your property value by keeping the property well-maintained. Make the association work for you.

4

YOUR CAR

HOW TO BUY A NEW CAR

Buying a new car can bring fear and apprehension. Many new car buyers make the mistake of being overly concerned about a single aspect of buying a car. Their focus may be on the monthly payments or the trade-in allowance.

This kind of shortsightedness tends to leave the wallet a little flat. Here are some tips on buying a car.

First, determine what you would like your monthly car payment to be and for how long. The mistake most people make is in first finding a car they like, then trying to get the monthly payment to fit the budget.

As a rule, you should plan on spending not more than 10 percent of your gross monthly income on a car payment. So if you make $30,000 a year, your monthly payment should not be more than $250. This amount will determine how much car you will be able to buy. To car shop wisely, decide that you will spend, for example, no more than the $250 per month for 36 months.

Where Should You Get Your Loan?

Choosing where to get your loan is as important as deciding what car you buy. First, find out the value of the car you now own. Clean it up, take it to several used car dealers, and tell them you want to sell it outright, without trading, and you want their best offer. The best offer is the one you will use as your car's wholesale value.

Next, it's on to see what bank, savings and loan, credit union, car dealer, or insurance company has the best interest rate for the term and amount of money you want to borrow. You will want to select the lending institution with the lowest annual percentage rate.

Ask the lender to compute how much a certain monthly payment will buy you. For example, a monthly payment of $250 will mean you will spend a total of $9,000, $7,000 of which will go to buy the car and $2,000 will be the interest. The $7,000 is called the loan cash.

Determining the amount of equity you have in your car is simple. Subtract the amount you owe on the car from its wholesale value. If the wholesale value is $7,000 and you owe $3,000, your equity is $4,000 (see fig. 4.1).

Next, you want to figure your available cash. This is the amount of your loan cash plus the equity in the car you plan to trade ($7,000 plus $4,000 equals $11,000 available cash).

Visiting several dealerships is next on the agenda. You want to look for autos that have a manufacturer's sticker price about 10 to 15 percent higher than your available cash.

Do not discuss price with any salesperson. Just find a few cars you like and drive them. Record the price of each item on the manufacturer's sticker and leave.

FIGURE 4.1

PURCHASING A CAR

What $250 monthly payment will buy
($9,000 3-year loan @ 15%)

$ 7,000	cash to buy car
$ 2,000	interest on loan
$ 9,000	total loan

The trade-in

$ 7,000	trade-in wholesale value
$ 3,000	balance on trade-in loan
$ 4,000	net cash for trade-in

Money available for new car

$ 7,000	cash to buy car from loan
$ 4,000	net cash from trade-in
$11,000	total available cash for new car purchase

Finding How Much the Dealer Paid for the Car

Using a new auto price guide can help determine the cost of the car (and every item on the sticker) to the dealer. These guides are available at many bookstores and most libraries. Some popular ones are from *Consumer Reports* magazine and *Edmund's Car Price* guides. You can order a printout for the make and model that you want to buy. The printout will show you the suggested retail price of the car and how much the dealer paid for it, along with the wholesale and retail cost of options such as power steering, AM/FM radio, and so on.

The total dealer cost has a profit of 2 to 3 percent built in. Experts say that 5 to 12 percent over the dealer cost is fair, depending on the price of the car.

Your maximum offer will be less than your available cash

because you want to allow for sales tax and maintenance charges. Write down your offer, and subtract the wholesale value of your present car. Armed with all this ammunition, you are now ready to make an appointment to talk with a salesperson.

Negotiating the Deal

Negotiating to buy a car means being prepared. Knowing the amount of money you plan to spend and the dealer's cost of your dream car, you are now ready to wheel and deal. Ask the salesperson for a wholesale appraisal of your car, not an allowance figure. Keep in mind the wholesale figures you got from the used car dealers. If the person agrees on your figure, write it down.

Make an offer on the new car that is less than the maximum offer you are willing to make. That way, you give the salesperson room to negotiate.

Once you have agreed on a figure, write it down. Deduct the trade-in offer from the agreed car price. If the figure is acceptable, tell the salesperson to write up a buyer's order.

After the deal is approved by the manager, sign the order and give a small deposit if requested. And perhaps for the first time you will better understand what it takes to get a good deal on a new car.

HOW TO READ CAR STICKER PRICES

Lowballing is the practice of quoting a very low price to entice potential auto buyers. The key to paying a price close to the lowball is to understand how cars are priced.

The sticker price is the manufacturer's best guess about the fair value of the car, and it includes the markup over the dealer's cost for the car. This markup can run from 4 to 25 percent.

The base price, the price posted in the ads, appears at the top of a federally required sticker. Prices that appear below the base price are manufacturer-installed options.

In some cases, dealers have their own sticker that includes dealer-installed options such as air-conditioning and tape players and other items of dubious value like undercoating.

To cut the price, negotiate the price of these extra items, or eliminate them. Remember, the sticker price has a profit for the dealer already built in.

EXTENDED SERVICE CONTRACTS

Should you buy a service contract on your new car? Many car dealers offer extended service contracts that you can buy for a fee. These contracts promise to pay for repairs that are not covered by the manufacturer's regular warranty.

A service contract generally covers only critical drive-train components and internal engine problems. The original manufacturer's warranty should cover these items.

When you consider a service contract, make sure the coverage does not duplicate the manufacturer's warranty. Many car companies now have coverage that extends up to five or six years or sixty thousand miles.

Any serious defects in your car will develop within the normal warranty period. So buying a service contract may not make sense unless it will cover the car beyond the original warranty, and unless you plan to keep the car more than four or five years.

HOW TO BUY CAR INSURANCE

Careful shopping will uncover bargains in car insurance (see fig. 4.2). Car insurance rates continue to climb as inflation is subdued. Last year the inflation rate was about 3 percent, while car insurance has gone up 55 percent over the last five years. It pays to periodically review your coverage to see that it's adequate, not excessive or overpriced.

In a recent survey, insurance companies were asked for rates on a policy covering a husband, a wife, and a seventeen-year-old son living in a northeastern city, all with flawless driving records. The highest yearly premium was more than $1,400, while the lowest was almost $600.

The drastic differences were attributed to several factors, including marketing methods and the amount of commissions paid to agents. If you are patient and willing to invest time, you can find a policy that fits your needs and your wallet.

Car Insurance and Liability Coverage

Liability protection is a vital part of your car insurance. Making sure you have enough liability coverage can save you from financial disaster.

If you injure somebody and are found liable, your liability insurance pays for the victim's medical and hospital expenses, rehabilitation, nursing care, lost income, and "pain and suffering."

Your coverage is good only up to the policy limits. You can be held personally responsible for any excess that the insurance does not cover.

Liability coverage is mandatory in most states, and typical coverage is $25,000 per person, $50,000 per accident bodily

Figure 4.2

AUTO INSURANCE

Auto insurance is the type of insurance you are most likely to own. Most states require licensed drivers who own cars to be insured. Your exposure to liability is enormously high when you drive a car, and instead of just getting the minimum insurance required by the state, you should carefully determine the coverage you need. Use the worksheet and explanation below.

Feature	Recommendation	Policy 1 Coverage	Annual Premium Cost	Policy 2 Coverage	Annual Premium Cost
1. Bodily injury liability and property damage	100/300/50 (at least)	________	________	________	________
2. Medical payments	$25,000	________	________	________	________
3. Uninsured/ underinsured motorist	100/300/50	________	________	________	________
4. Collision	Highest deductible you can handle	________	________	________	________
5. Comprehensive	Highest deductible you can handle	________	________	________	________
6. Towing and/or rental	Optional	________	________	________	________
TOTAL PREMIUM COST			$________		$________

HOW TO FILL OUT THE WORKSHEET

1. Bodily injury liability and property damage. The injury portion covers anyone other than yourself for injuries caused by you. Covered expenses are medical payments, rehabilitation expenses, lost income, and compensation for pain and suffering. The property portion protects against damage to somebody else's property, such as automobile, landscaping, or home. Most insurance experts recommend minimum levels of 25/50/10. These numbers represent $25,000 injury to one person in an accident; maximum of $50,000 per accident for injuries; and $10,000 damage to property. You should, however, consider at least 100/300/50; if you can afford it or you have substantial assets to protect, consider 250/500 for bodily injury.

2. Medical payments. This covers medical expenses for you and your passengers for a defined period, usually a year. You might want it because your passengers might not have coverage of their own. Recommended limit is $25,000.

3. Uninsured/underinsured motorist. This covers you, your family, and your passengers if you are injured by a hit-and-run driver or if the other driver has no or inadequate insurance. Recommended limits are 100/300/50.

4. Collision. Collision insurance pays for damage to your car if an accident is your fault or if an at-fault driver doesn't have insurance. It can be very expensive and is not usually worth the cost if your car is older. Coverage is only for the depreciated value of your car. If coverage costs 10 percent or more of the car's value, or if your car is more than five years old, you probably should not have it, but some lenders may require it.

5. Comprehensive. This pays for most other types of damage, such as theft, vandalism, or storm damage. Coverage recommendation is the same as for collision.

6. Towing and/or rental. This pays for towing your car from the site of an accident or for renting a car if yours is stolen or in an accident. Coverage is cheap, but you might already have it from an auto club or in your collision or comprehensive coverage.

injury, and $10,000 for property damage. This is usually stated as 25/50/10.

Insurance experts insist that this coverage is not sufficient. They state that minimums of $100,000 per person, $300,000 per accident, and $50,000 for property damage are more realistic.

Ways to Save Money

If you are willing to take on just $200 worth of risk, you may save money on your collision and comprehensive coverage.

Collision insurance pays for damage to your car if an accident is your fault or if an at-fault driver doesn't have insurance. Comprehensive insurance protects you against fire, theft, vandalism, and other disasters.

The key to saving money on collision and comprehensive is the deductible—how much you are willing to pay before the insurance takes over. Deductibles for this type of coverage generally range between $50 and $500. The higher the deductible, the lower the premium.

You may be wise to choose the highest deductible you can afford to pay without seriously disrupting your finances.

Save Money with Optional Coverages

By eliminating or minimizing certain types of optional coverage, you can save money on car insurance.

If you have high-limit health insurance, you may not want no-fault or medical payments coverage. No-fault coverage is mandatory in many states but optional in others. It pays medical expenses regardless of who is at fault. Medical payments coverage is similar but optional in many states, also. No-fault or medical payments coverage could help if your health insurance is not enough.

Another way to save is by evaluating your uninsured motorist and underinsured motorist insurance. Both pay for injury losses, and in some states for property damage, if you're in an accident with an at-fault driver who has no insurance or too little insurance.

Save Money with Discounts

You may qualify for special discounts on your auto insurance. When you're shopping for auto insurance, ask each company to provide a list of the discounts available in addition to the amount you will have to pay for the coverage you want.

Discounts of up to 40 percent are available for good driving. The requirements may vary, but you may qualify if you haven't had any moving violations or chargeable accidents in the last thirty-six months. A course in driver training or defensive driving may also lower your premiums. If your car has air bags or automatic safety belts, your premium may be lowered. A few companies have lower premiums for nonsmokers and drivers who don't drink.

If you consolidate your coverage with one company by insuring more than one vehicle, you may be eligible for a discount. Make sure you get at least three quotes from several insurance companies as you shop, and check with your current insurance agent before making any changes.

LEASING A CAR

If high car prices and huge down payments are scaring you away from automobile showrooms, consider leasing a car. There are two basic types of leases—closed-end and open-end.

In a closed-end lease, you pay a monthly fee for the term of the contract and turn in the car at the end of the lease. The term is usually not more than five years. Your monthly payments are based on the mileage you expect to put on the car. The more you drive, the higher the monthly fee. If you exceed the agreed-upon mileage, you pay extra. Your monthly payments may cover routine maintenance, which includes tune-ups, oil changes, and wheel alignments.

In general, closed-end leases are more expensive than open-end leases, but they are better suited for someone who plans to put a lot of mileage on a car and would rather not buy it at the end of the lease.

With an open-end lease, the option to buy the car at the end of the lease sets the purchase price in advance. This amount represents the dealer's estimated resale value at the end of the lease.

The resale value is calculated by consulting current data from banks and the *Kelly Blue Book*, an industry-wide guide. At the end of the lease, if the purchase price of the car as stated in the lease agreement is less than what you would have to pay to buy it in the used car market, you indeed have a bargain.

However, if you decide not to purchase the car and opt instead to trade it in, a new appraisal will be ordered, and you will have to settle up with the dealer.

Settling Up with the Dealer

In an open-end lease, if you prefer not to buy the car at the end of the contract, a new appraisal is done. You and the dealer will settle up in one of three ways.

First, if the car is worth exactly what the dealer predicted, you owe nothing. Second, if the car is worth more than the dealer predicted, he owes you money. Third, if the car is worth less than the dealer calculated, you owe him part of the difference. Under the Consumer Leasing Act, this amount is usually not more than three times the monthly payments.

The option to buy the car at the end of the lease is an incentive to get you to treat it like your own. Under the current tax law, finance charges on consumer loans are not tax-deductible, so leasing may be a better alternative.

What to Ask the Dealer

It's more important to examine the deal rather than the dealer when it comes to leasing a car. Any firm that leases you a car is required by the Consumer Leasing Act to tell you the costs you might incur. These costs include the size of your monthly payments, who is responsible for insurance on the vehicle, and what the car's estimated resale value will be at the end of the lease.

Other facts you will want explained are late payment fees, the cost of canceling the lease, and how wear and tear will be determined. The law says that standards of measurement must be "reasonable."

If your preference for expensive cars is long and your cash is short, leasing can put you behind the wheel of a rich person's car. And who's to know you're renting it?

TRADE-INS

Many people trade in the old car when they buy a new one, but that may not be the best way. You may get a better price for the old car if you try to sell it yourself.

The first step is to find out what your old car is worth. For a rough idea, check the classified section of your local newspaper. You want to find out what other people are asking for the same make and model as your car. You should also check the car's "book value" by getting a copy of the *National Association of Automobile Dealers' Official Used Car Guide*. This book is updated monthly and lists trade-in and retail prices for most used cars. You will find a copy at the library or your bank.

The prices you see in the guide are benchmarks. The trade-in price is what you could expect to be offered by a dealer for a car in good condition with average mileage. The retail price is roughly what the dealer would charge for the car.

When you're ready to sell the old car, make sure it looks as good as you can make it. Don't repair major dents. But do make minor repairs; for example, touch up the paint and replace trim. Get some routine maintenance done, such as oil change, tune-up, and so on. Don't forget to have the car washed and waxed and the interior cleaned. It may pay to take your car to a company that specializes in automotive detailing.

Negotiating the Trade-In

If you decide to trade in your car at a dealer, treat the trade-in as a separate transaction. Don't tie the trade-in to your negotiations over the price of the new car.

If the dealer offers you much less than the book value, ask why the offer is so low. If you can't agree on a price, consider selling the car privately.

Selling the Car Yourself

Making a private sale will involve much more bother than trading in at the dealer. If you are not able to sell the car to a relative or friend, you will have to advertise the car. Keep in mind that you will have to take phone calls and reserve time to show the car. Of course, the reward for all of this extra work is that you have a greater chance of selling the car for the price you want.

A couple of reminders: don't promise more than the car can deliver, and don't surrender the title until you have the cash in hand. You might wish to ask for a certified check or a money order for the full price.

COLLISION DAMAGE WAIVER

You can't win with rental car insurance. Do you really need to sign up for collision damage waiver coverage? Whenever you rent a car, the agent tries to get you to sign up for the collision damage waiver (CDW). This coverage pays for damages to the car if you are in an accident.

Typically, this coverage costs $9 to $10 per day. It has been estimated that auto insurers could provide the same protection for as little as $3 a year.

No matter what the agent says, you probably don't need the coverage. At least 60 percent of all private auto insurance policies provide coverage when you rent a car. Check with your insurance agent before renting.

Some gold credit cards even provide CDW automatically when you use the card to rent a car. But even with your own coverage, you're not home free. The rental car company can still hold you responsible for damage in an accident.

If you have an accident, the car rental company can charge you with a repair charge estimate on your credit card bill. But there is help on the way.

The National Association of Insurance Commissioners is calling for state laws that would require rental companies to provide CDW automatically and to include the cost in their advertised rates. Competition would help keep the cost down. But for now, you're on your own.

Purchase CDW if you're driving in a high-risk area or if you don't want to risk filing a claim on your own policy, which could raise your rates.

PAYING A FAIR PRICE FOR CAR REPAIRS

If you recently had some work done on your car, you probably wondered if car repair costs are getting out of hand. Well, they are, but you can fight back if you know how to get a fair price.

At the least, you have to know how repair shops set their prices. They take three factors into consideration. First, the mechanic's hourly rate, which can range from $40 to $70 an hour. Second, the cost of the parts, including a markup. And third, the time it takes to do the job.

Car repair shops, including dealerships, consult manuals like *Mitchell's Parts and Labor Estimating Book* to determine how much time a repair should take. So, if it takes two hours to install a fuel pump and the dealer uses a $50-an-hour labor rate, the repair will cost you $100 in labor, not including the cost of the part.

How to Get a Good Deal

To find out if you are paying a fair price, search your library for a copy of a flat-rate manual, like *Mitchell's*, which lists how long certain repairs should take. Then call around to the parts stores to find out the retail price for the part you want repaired. Using an average of $50 an hour for labor, find out what the total bill should come to. Then call several car repair shops and get estimates.

After you select a repair shop to make the repairs, make sure you get *written* estimates that include how long the job will take and how much parts will cost. Ask questions about estimates that are out of line with your research.

When you take in your car to be repaired, tell the mechanic you want all the old parts.

5

YOUR CREDIT

CREDIT—HOW TO CUT YOUR DEBT

Credit. We all need it sooner or later. In a country that has seen the total consumer debt grow to more than $600 billion, credit is power. The proper use of credit enables you to have a standard of living that your parents only dreamed of. But abusing credit will turn the best-laid financial plans into a nightmare.

Borrowing used to make sense. You could deduct interest payments on consumer debt from income taxes. Now, interest charges on your consumer debt are no longer deductible. The average American family owes $1,600 in unpaid revolving credit. The escalating broad use of credit has resulted in a consumer in credit trouble and in need of help.

How to Tell If You're in Credit Trouble

The first steps toward getting out of debt are actually the most obvious and the most difficult ones to take. Admit that you have a problem, then stop borrowing.

Determine how much debt you have. List all the unpaid balances you owe (see fig. 5.1), add them up, and ask yourself, Can I pay them off in one year?

In addition, look at what you pay each month. If your monthly debt payments equal 15 percent or more of your after-tax income, excluding your mortgage payment, you're in over your head.

FIGURE 5.1

LIST OF DEBTS

Creditor	Type of Loan	Date of Last Payment	Maturity Date	Monthly Payment	Total Amount Owed
______	______	______	______	$______	$______
______	______	______	______	______	______
______	______	______	______	______	______
______	______	______	______	______	______
______	______	______	______	______	______
______	______	______	______	______	______
______	______	______	______	______	______
______	______	______	______	______	______
______	______	______	______	______	______
______	______	______	______	______	______
		TOTAL MONTHLY PAYMENTS		$______	
			TOTAL AMOUNT OWED		$______

Here are some other telltale signs of credit trouble:

- You pay the minimum amounts or less each month on your charge cards.
- You've reached your credit limits.

- You no longer contribute to a savings account, or you have no savings at all.
- Creditors are sending you past due notices.

If some of these problems sound familiar, you're in trouble. *But there is a way out.*

What to Do to Get Out of Credit Trouble

First of all, don't panic. Do your best to live on cash, pay off what you owe, and concentrate on changing your spending habits.

Instead of defining credit in terms of minimum monthly payments, look at total outstanding balances. If you have to continue to charge on your accounts, pay off all new charges on your accounts and the interest, and try to pay off a portion of the previous month's balance.

Next, develop a budget. Most people who avoid excess debt budget their money. A budget is a snapshot of where your money goes when it leaves your hands. To help balance your budget, you may have to cut some expenses. Maybe you're carrying too much insurance. Consider a second or temporary job to generate additional income and help pay off the debt.

Where to Get Help

If your credit problems become so severe that you need professional advice, there are 356 nonprofit consumer credit counseling services nationwide whose advice is available free of charge or for a small fee. Credit counseling centers are often better able than you are to negotiate with creditors for greater concessions on interest rates, fees, and penalties. These centers also conduct seminars teaching the wise use of credit. You can contact the Consumer Credit Counseling Service at

1-800-388-CCCS for the name and location of the CCCS office near you.

Beware of private credit repair centers. You should approach them with caution. Their fees are often high, and the promised credit "fix" may not be possible. If you are considering such a service, make sure you get what spokespersons say they will do for you and how much it will cost in writing.

In addition, check the references of the center with previous clients. Remember, using credit wisely is one of the keys to managing your finances.

YOUR CREDIT REPORT

One of the more interesting parts of your credit history is not what is on your credit report (see fig. 5.2) but what is not. You may be disappointed or relieved to know that your rent, utility bills, and doctor and lawyer fees are often not reported. But new areas are always being added to the list of reported items. Until recently, American Express did not report negative information to credit bureaus. Now the company does report negative data and positive data when requested.

Interpreting your report can be a challenge. Some bureaus use a system called common language, which ranks bill-paying style on a scale from one to nine. The rating is supplied by the creditor, not the credit agency. Number one is the best rating, indicating you pay your bills on time within thirty days or as agreed. The worst rating is a nine, which indicates bad debt, placed for collection or bankruptcy.

How to Correct Errors in Your Credit Report

The credit bureau gathers the information in your credit file. What is in your file is the result of reports from lenders.

Some information the bureau receives can be wrong. To correct mistakes, inform the bureau in writing. Any time you dispute an item, the credit bureau must investigate. If it cannot verify the facts by going back to the original source, the information must be deleted.

If the information is accurate, but there are certain facts about the situation you want known, you can write your version of the incident. This document then becomes part of your record and must be shown to all lenders who request your file.

Credit is a double-edged sword. It can be the instrument for increased financial problems or for a more abundant life-style.

BANKRUPTCY—THE LAST RESORT

Filing for bankruptcy is a serious step and will affect your financial health for years to come. There is no formula for determining when your debt has reached a level where bankruptcy is the best route to relief of a financial crisis.

Bankruptcy is a legal declaration of your inability to pay your debts. It stays on your credit record for ten years. Trying to get credit after filing bankruptcy is nearly impossible.

If you have already considered debt counseling and even a consolidation loan with no success, bankruptcy may be the only option left. You should consider it only when you have exhausted every means possible to work out a repayment plan with your creditors. There are two types of personal bankruptcy: Chapter 13 and Chapter 7. Chapter 13 reorganization is the less drastic of the two.

Chapter 13—a Milder Form of Bankruptcy

In a Chapter 13 filing, you will pay all or part of your debt while keeping your home and some of your other property.

FIGURE 5.2

UPDATED CREDIT PROFILE

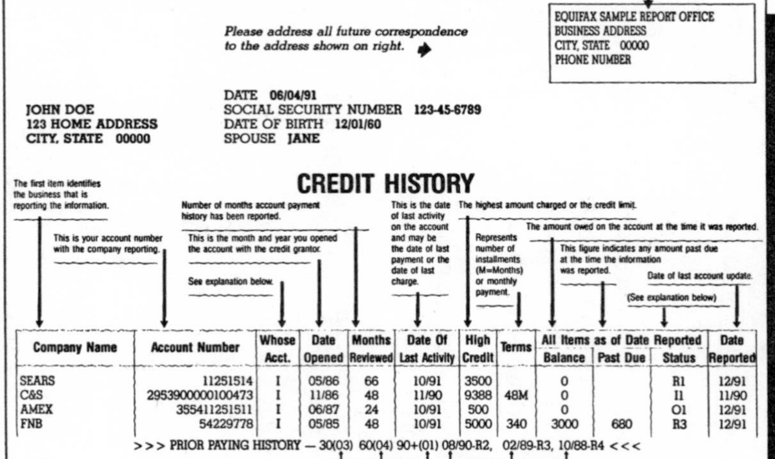

EQUIFAX *The Information Source*

CREDIT INFORMATION SERVICES

Sample Credit Report

The Name and Address of the Equifax office you should contact if you have any questions or disagreement with your credit report.

EQUIFAX SAMPLE REPORT OFFICE
BUSINESS ADDRESS
CITY, STATE 00000
PHONE NUMBER

Please address all future correspondence to the address shown on right.

I.D. Section
Your name, current address and other identifying information reported by your creditors.

JOHN DOE
123 HOME ADDRESS
CITY, STATE 00000

DATE 06/04/91
SOCIAL SECURITY NUMBER 123-45-6789
DATE OF BIRTH 12/01/60
SPOUSE JANE

Credit History Section
List of open and paid accounts indicating any late payments reported by your creditors.

CREDIT HISTORY

The first item identifies the business that is reporting the information.

This is your account number with the company reporting.

Number of months account payment history has been reported.

This is the month and year you opened the account with the credit grantor.

See explanation below.

This is the date of last activity on the account and may be the date of last payment or the date of last charge.

The highest amount charged or the credit limit.

Represents number of installments (M=Months) or monthly payment.

The amount owed on the account at the time it was reported.

This figure indicates any amount past due at the time the information was reported.

Date of last account update.

(See explanation below)

Company Name	Account Number	Whose Acct.	Date Opened	Months Reviewed	Date Of Last Activity	High Credit	Terms	All Items as of Date Reported: Balance	Past Due	Status	Date Reported
SEARS	11251514	I	05/86	66	10/91	3500		0		R1	12/91
C&S	2953900000100473	I	11/86	48	11/90	9388	48M	0		I1	11/90
AMEX	355411251511	I	06/87	24	10/91	500		0		O1	12/91
FNB	54229778	I	05/85	48	10/91	5000	340	3000	680	R3	12/91

>>> PRIOR PAYING HISTORY — 30(03) 60(04) 90+(01) 08/90-R2, 02/89-R3, 10/88-R4 <<<

Number of times account was either 30/60/90 days past due.

Date two most recent delinquencies occurred plus date of most severe delinquency.

Collection Accounts
Accounts which your creditors turned over to a collection agency.

COLLECTION ACCOUNTS

>>> COLLECTION REPORTED 06/90, ASSIGNED TO PRO COLL 09/89, CLIENT-ABC HOSP AMOUNT-$978, UNPAID 06/90, BALANCE-$978 06/90 DATE OF LAST ACTIVITY 09/89, INDIVIDUAL, ACCOUNT NUMBER 787652JC

Courthouse Records
Public Record items obtained from local, state and federal courts which reflect your history of meeting financial obligations.

COURTHOUSE RECORDS

>>> LIEN FILED 03/88, FULTON CTY, CASE NUMBER-32114, AMOUNT-$26667, CLASS-CITY/COUNTY RELEASED 07/88, VERIFIED 09/90

>>> BANKRUPTCY FILED 12/89, FULTON CTY, CASE NUMBER-673HC12, LIABILITIES-$15787, PERSONAL INDIVIDUAL, DISCHARGED, ASSETS-$780

AMOUNT-$8984, PLAINTIFF-ABC REAL ESTATE, SATISFIED 03/89, VERIFIED 05/90

ADDITIONAL INFORMATION

>>>FORMER ADDRESS 456 JUPITER, RD, ATLANTA, GA 30245

>>>FORMER ADDRESS P. O. BOX 2138, SAVANNAH, GA 31406

>>>CURRENT EMPLOYMENT ENGINEER, SPACE PATROL

INQUIRY SECTION

.... COMPANIES THAT REQUESTED YOUR CREDIT HISTORY ....

06/04/91	EQUIFAX	06/03/90	GECC	08/30/89	MACYS
05/03/91	VISA	04/01/90	FIRST NATL	07/03/89	RICHS
02/13/91	SEARS	03/05/90	PRM VISA	06/20/91	C&S
01/23/91	JC PENNEY	01/03/90	SPEIGEL	06/03/91	FAMILY FIN

INQUIRIES NOT REPORTED TO CUSTOMERS

A PRM inquiry means that only your name and address were given to a credit grantor so they could offer you an application for credit.

An A/M or AR inquiry indicates a periodic review of your credit history by one of your creditors.

An Equifax inquiry indicates our activity in response to your request for a copy of your credit report.

PRM, AM, AR and Equifax inquiries do not show on credit reports that businesses receive, only on reports provided to you.

Additional Information

Primarily consists of former addresses and employments reported by your creditors.

Inquiry Section

List of businesses that have received your credit report in the last 24 months.

Whose Account

Indicates who is responsible for the account and the type of participation you have with the account.

- **J** = Joint
- **I** = Individual
- **U** = Undesignated
- **A** = Authorized user
- **T** = Terminated
- **M** = Maker
- **C** = Co-Maker/Co-Signer
- **B** = On behalf of another person
- **S** = Shared

Status

Type Of Account

- **O** = Open (entire balance due each month)
- **R** = Revolving (payment amount variable)
- **I** = Installment (fixed number of payments)

Timeliness Of Payment

- **0** = Approved not used
- **1** = Paid as agreed
- **2** = 30 days past due
- **3** = 60 days past due
- **4** = 90 days past due
- **5** = 120 days past due
- **7** = Making regular payments under wage earner plan or similar arrangement
- **8** = Repossesion
- **9** = Seriously delinquent/bad debt (paid or unpaid)

Length Of Time Information Remains In Your File

Credit and collection accounts — 7 years from date of last activity with original creditor.

Courthouse records— 7 years from date filed except Bankruptcy chapters 7 and 11 which remain for 10 years from date filed.

Note: New York State only. Satisified judgments 5 years from the date filed. Paid collections 5 years from date of last activity with original creditor.

Chapter 13 is called the wage earner plan because it protects your wages and essential property.

Here's how it works. Your creditors are invited to participate in a plan to restructure your debt. A written agreement is prepared and may include a reduction in the amount you owe each creditor, in addition to lengthening the repayment schedule. This plan results in lower monthly payments. Legal fees associated with bankruptcy can range from $500 to $1,500. You also have to pay filing fees and trustee's fees.

Chapter 7—the Final Solution

Chapter 7 bankruptcy is the more drastic and severe approach to ending a debt situation. Unlike Chapter 13, which allows you to restructure your debt, in a Chapter 7 procedure the court takes most of what you own, converts it to cash, and divides it among your creditors. You keep up to $20,000 equity in your home, car, and other property, and you get to start over.

Filing personal bankruptcy will not eliminate taxes, alimony, child support, or educational loans. A Chapter 7 filing can cost up to $750, in addition to court costs and other fees.

Bankruptcy remains a part of your credit record for ten years; any unpaid debt remains there indefinitely. Bankruptcy is not cheap, but if you are facing financial disaster, it offers a way out.

CREDIT CARD SECRETS

When your funds get low, you need to know which bills you can put off paying without damaging your credit rating. Debts charged against credit cards issued by department stores such as Sears should be paid immediately.

Bank credit cards (e.g., VISA and MasterCard) should also

be among the first in line to be paid each and every month. These institutions submit reports on all customers to credit-reporting agencies every month. The reports often date back as long as two years.

Oil companies and utilities would be less likely to file a report to a credit bureau. Doctors and hospitals don't file reports with credit-reporting bureaus, either. So in a money crunch, you can postpone paying them, and it's less likely to affect your credit rating. But remember, you still need to be responsible and pay all your bills on time.

What VISA and MasterCard Don't Tell You

The MasterCard and VISA organizations do not issue credit cards. They provide a clearing system for charges and payments on their cards. They license banks to use the VISA and MasterCard names.

The issuing bank determines the interest rates and fees. A recently discovered loophole in the federal law allows federally chartered out-of-state banks to ignore state laws that limit interest and fees on credit cards.

That means if your state has a law limiting the interest charged on credit cards to 10 percent, an out-of-state bank may be able to issue a credit card in your state and charge more than the 10 percent limit. That's why your credit card agreement will have different interest rates depending on which state you live in or the state from which it was issued.

Advantages of Credit Card Purchases

What are some advantages of paying by credit card? Retail stores for the most part have liberal return policies, but most mechanics, mail-order houses, and other vendors do not. Paying an auto mechanic by credit card will protect you from sloppy or unnecessary work.

Vendors understand that in the case of a dispute over a service or a product, you can withhold payment when the credit card bill arrives. The procedure is quite simple. First, make your complaint known, and try to settle the dispute. If that doesn't work, send a letter to the credit card company and the business explaining why the service or product was unsatisfactory. Under the Fair Credit Billing Act, the credit card company cannot force you to pay until the matter is resolved. Check your credit card agreement for details about when this procedure can be used.

The Best Time to Charge on a Credit Card

Make credit card purchases on or just before the cutoff date. The average processing for a purchase takes a couple of days. The purchase will show up not on your next statement but on the following one.

This method gives you a float of about fifty days. Check your statement to find the cutoff date. It usually falls around the same time each month.

Credit cards are most costly when used for a cash advance. You get no float on these transactions, and the interest rate is higher than that charged for purchases. Shop around, and use only credit cards that charge low interest rates. Banks in Oregon, Delaware, and Arkansas offer some of the lowest rates.

Price Protection

With consumers now holding many different credit cards in their wallets, banks have become more aggressive with their credit card advertising in an effort to get you to use theirs. A new feature offered by some banks that issue credit cards is called price protection. Here's how it works. If you buy an item with the bank's credit card and then see the same item advertised in print for a lower price within sixty days of your purchase, the bank will refund the difference up to a certain dollar amount. For example, if you purchase a pair of shoes with the credit card for $100 and then see the same pair of shoes in a printed ad for only $75, the bank will refund to you the difference of $25.

THE BEST LOANS FOR LESS

Changing the way you borrow money could be the smartest move you make. The days of high inflation and tax-deductible interest are a memory. The new world of credit requires you to rethink the way you borrow money. The new rules of debt, plus heated competition for your borrowing needs, make the time ripe for a fresh review of your credit strategy.

Mailboxes are being stuffed with offers for credit cards. Homeowners are being solicited for home equity lines of credit and unsecured loans. Consumer installment debt, not counting mortgages, has reached an all-time high of more than 19 percent of disposable income.

The idea that consumers are deeply burdened is questionable. Personal bankruptcies are at a record high, but mortgage delinquencies are down.

The elimination of the deductibility of interest charges on loans means the wise use of credit will save you money.

Credit Cards

Selecting the right credit card can save you money (see fig. 5.3). High credit card interest rates and the loss of interest rate deductions have failed to put a damper on credit card use. If you're going to use the card, you'll need to know three things.

First is the interest rate. The average credit card rate is

about 18 percent. But in a recent survey, rates as low as 10.50 percent were found in some states. If you will be using a lot of revolving credit and making only the minimum payment, choose a card with a low APR (annual percentage rate). For a

FIGURE 5.3

CREDIT CARD COMPARISON SHOPPING

How does your credit card stack up? This figure shows current rates and other provisions for the average card and the best card available. In the column at right, you can plug in your card's vital statistics.

	Average Card	Best Card	Your Card
Annual percentage rate:			
Regular cards	18.6%	14.0%	________
Gold cards	17.5%	13.0%	________
Annual fee:			
Regular cards	$18.50	none	________
Gold cards	$38.60	none	________
Grace period	25 days	30 days	________
Grace period includes new purchases?	no	yes	________
Cash advance transaction fee (percentage of loan)	1%–2%	none	________

Interest rates are for cards with no membership fee; some cards with membership fees have somewhat lower rates.

list of banks with the lowest rates, write to the Bankcard Holders of America (BHA), 560 Herndon Parkway, Suite 120, Herndon, Virginia 22070.

Second is the annual fee. The average fee charged is just a little more than $17, but you can still find plenty of cards that are free. If you pay off your balance each month, you should shop for the best annual fee deal. The BHA also offers a list of cards with no fee.

Third is the grace period. Usually, you will get a month between the day you charge a purchase and the day the interest charges start stacking up. Some cards have no grace period. If you intend to pay your balances in full, be sure your card has a grace period.

Home Mortgages

Getting the best mortgage loan means deciding whether to get a fixed or an adjustable rate and for how long. Tax reform left mortgage interest deductions intact but diminished the value of the deduction by lowering tax brackets.

There are still attractive choices if you are shopping for a mortgage, whether its rate is fixed or adjustable. With a fixed-rate mortgage, the interest rate stays the same during the life of the loan, whereas the rate on an adjustable loan may change. With projections of steady or declining interest rates for the next decade or so, adjustable-rate mortgages may be the better deal, provided the rate is at least two percentage points less than a fixed-rate mortgage.

A $50,000 loan at 9 percent for thirty years would cost about $400 per month, and the same loan for fifteen years would have monthly payments of approximately $500. Over the life of the loan, the fifteen-year mortgage would save you almost $38,000 in mortgage payments.

Auto Loans

Shopping smart for a car loan will keep you in the driver's seat. The tough and well-informed negotiator will come out ahead. Shopping for an auto loan should be a separate activity from shopping for a car whenever possible.

Many banks and other financial institutions have responded aggressively to manufacturers' cut-rate financing, with highly competitive loans of their own.

If you are offered a choice between cut-rate financing and a cash rebate, ask the dealer to run the numbers for both deals. Often taking the rebate and getting the loan somewhere else mean a better deal.

Shorter loans will also save you money even though they mean higher monthly payments. A $10,000 four-year loan at 11 percent will have monthly payments of $258. The same loan for only two years will require payments of $466 per month. However, with the two-year loan, you will save more than $1,200 in interest charges.

Borrow from Yourself

Finding the best loan may mean borrowing money from yourself. Since the government no longer subsidizes your borrowing needs through interest deductions, developing a credit strategy can be a challenge. Meet that challenge by borrowing from yourself.

You can borrow against the cash value of your life insurance policy, with older policies having interest rates of 5 to 6 percent. In some cases, you don't have to pay back the loan. If you die with a loan outstanding, the debt is subtracted from the face value before the proceeds are paid out.

Another relatively cheap source of credit is a loan secured

by your savings account or certificate of deposit. Many banks and some savings and loans offer such loans at 2 to 3 percent above the rate they're paying on your money; that means a loan in the 7.5 to 10 percent range. Your money continues to earn interest but cannot be withdrawn as long as the debt is outstanding.

6

YOUR TAXES

YOUR TAX ADVISOR

During the January to April tax season, most advisors are too busy to take on new clients. If you hire a tax pro early, you may be able to cut your tax bill this year.

There are basically four types of practitioners. *Tax preparers* who work for storefront chains such as H & R Block can handle simple returns.

If you are self-employed and invest regularly, a *certified public accountant* (CPA) or an *enrolled agent* may be more suitable. Make sure the CPA specializes in taxes; not all do. Enrolled agents have worked for the IRS five years or have passed a demanding two-day IRS test. CPAs and enrolled agents provide tax-planning advice as well as prepare tax returns.

The final option is a *tax lawyer* whose services would be absolutely necessary when facing a divorce or dealing with a will that requires tax and legal advice.

Choosing Your Tax Advisor

A good tax practitioner will save you more money than the professional will cost you. The best way to find one is through a referral from a friend or family member. Look for someone who matches your temperament. Some people favor a conservative approach to taxes while others prefer a tax practitioner who is more aggressive and willing to suggest write-offs that may be denied by the IRS.

Whatever approach you take with your taxes, make sure you talk with your tax practitioner at least three times a year—in the fall to discuss your tax bill due in April; in January to turn over your tax records for preparation of your return; and after the return is completed to find further ways to reduce your tax bill.

You should discuss with your advisor any plans for a major investment decision, such as buying or selling real estate, and for significant changes in your life, such as marriage or divorce.

KNOW YOUR TAX LAWS

One of the best ways to stay on top of your financial affairs is to know the tax laws and keep records of your transactions. The basics include knowing your tax bracket. Then you can determine how a tax transaction will affect you. For example, if you are in the 15 percent tax bracket, you will save approximately $150 for every $1,000 in deductions.

To become financially successful, you need a working knowledge of the tax laws and their impact on your personal or business transactions. Finding an accountant who can help you cut your tax bill is part of a strategy for achieving your financial goals. The goal is to pay only what the law requires.

Personal Exemptions

Tax planning is an important tool when it comes to minimizing your total tax bill. Part of the plan is to use as many deductions and exemptions as the law allows. You can deduct certain items from your total income before the government starts taking its percentage of your money.

A portion of your income that is exempt from taxes is called the personal exemption, and it is currently set at around $2,300. For each person in your family, including yourself, your spouse, children, and dependent parents, you get to deduct $2,300 before calculating your taxable income. So if you have a spouse and two children, you can deduct $9,200, four times $2,300.

Standard Deductions

A basic decision you will have to make before filing your taxes is determining whether to take the standard deduction or to itemize your deductions.

In general, you should take the standard deduction if that amount is more than the total itemized deductions you can claim. For tax year 1992, the standard deductions are $6,000 for married couples and $3,600 for single filers.

You should plan to itemize if you have large medical and dental expenses that are not covered by your insurance. Also, itemize if you paid taxes and mortgage interest on your home, and if you had large charitable deductions and certain moving and employee business expenses.

Making sure you qualify for the right deductions represents the principal means of saving money on your taxes.

Medical Expenses

In regard to medical expenses, the tax laws are fairly generous. But remember, you must spend money to take advantage of any tax deductions.

One category most people overlook is medical costs. You may want to take a closer look at your medical expenses if you added a new baby to the family or a family member had an extended hospital stay.

You are entitled to deduct medical expenses in excess of 7.5 percent of your adjusted gross income. Expenses that should be considered include out-of-pocket costs for doctors, dentists, and prescription drugs. In addition, you can deduct the costs of medical aids such as dentures, eyeglasses, and contact lenses. You can also deduct the cost of health insurance premiums. But if you're self-employed, you can deduct only 25 percent of your health insurance costs.

One Last Look

Some deductions are often overlooked. The federal government allows you to deduct income taxes you've paid to state and local governments. Real estate taxes are deductible on your federal income tax form. Also, your automobile registration fee may be deductible.

If you itemize, you can deduct contributions to your church, fraternity or sorority, or a private school or college. If you spend money for your job and your employer doesn't reimburse you, you may be able to claim a deduction for part of the costs. Items in this area include business lunches, union dues, uniforms, dues to professional organizations, subscriptions to professional journals, costs for a cellular phone, and a home computer.

HOW TO PREVENT AN IRS AUDIT

Nothing instills more fear in taxpayers than the thought of being audited by the Internal Revenue Service. Of the 96 million returns that are filed each year, only about 1.3 percent are singled out for the IRS's scrutiny, a fact the IRS is working to change.

For starters, the IRS has been adding more auditors to its payroll. The IRS is also working its way through a backlog of tax-shelter audits. Once auditors have cleared up the backlog, they may be turning their sights toward middle-income taxpayers who stretch an itemized deduction or two. All these actions can increase your chances of being audited by 60 percent. The average audit collects $4,000.

Audit-Proofing Your Tax Return

Some factors that are beyond our control determine who gets audited. For instance, if you earn more than $50,000 per year, you are ten times more likely to be audited than if you earn less than $10,000. If you are self-employed, the odds are even higher that the IRS will want to talk with you.

Most returns are singled out for an audit by an IRS computer program that gives numerical values to certain key items on your tax return. Your score is based on two things—how much the IRS believes you are likely to make an error when taking certain deductions, and how much your deduction varies from the average. The computer adds up the score on these individual items and assigns an overall score to your tax return. The higher the total score, the more likely you are to be audited.

What Triggers an Audit?

Some deductions on your tax return beg the IRS to audit you. For example, employee business expenses—labeled the "kiss of death" by IRS tax examiners—include deductions for a home office and business travel and entertainment.

Business use of your car that is out of line with your income will almost certainly result in an audit invitation. Most people just don't document these expenses, and the IRS knows it.

Charitable contributions merit a second look by the IRS. Cash contributions aren't likely to draw attention. But if you donate property, watch out! People tend to inflate the value of property they donate to charity.

Hobby losses for activities that seem more like pleasure than profit can definitely trigger an audit.

IRS Tax Penalties

In the past, investing in a tax shelter was a sure way to guarantee that the IRS would be giving your tax return closer scrutiny. But the possibility of an audit is even more likely if you fail to report income such as interest, dividends, and capital gains.

The IRS has become increasingly adept at matching the income information you give on your tax return to that supplied by banks and brokerage houses. Each year, millions of people receive notices saying that the income they reported didn't match the IRS's records. The IRS also can now match the records of those who pay alimony against those who receive it.

The consequences of cheating are becoming more and more unpleasant. For example, in the past if you didn't report interest or dividend income, you simply paid the tax plus interest. Now, on top of that, you could pay a negligent penalty.

Not only are the odds of getting caught going up, but so is the price.

CUT YOUR TAXES

You can do some last-minute things to get a bigger tax refund or pay less money to the IRS. For instance, double-check the W-2 form sent by your employer; mistakes do happen. If you find an error, notify your employer and the IRS. Fill out Form 4852 and attach it to your return.

Another tip is to include travel costs associated with your medical expenses. The cost of driving to and from a drugstore or the doctor's or dentist's office is deductible, as are charges for taxis, parking, and ambulances.

Don't forget the cost of contact lenses, which includes solutions, sterilizer, and insurance.

If you owe money to the IRS, sign your return and send it with your payment by registered mail. That way, you will be able to prove that you mailed the return on time.

LAST-MINUTE FILING TIPS

Tax reform has not thrown out all of your cherished deductions. There are still some choice "morsels" if you know where to look. Parents can still take a child-care credit for the cost of summer camp for children 13 and under, although overnight camp no longer qualifies.

If you own a home, check whether you can file as a "head of household," which has a lower tax rate. You can qualify if a child, grandchild, or stepchild lives with you but isn't your dependent. The rules are these: you must file a separate return; you must pay more than half the cost of upkeep for the home; and your home must have been the main residence of the child for more than six months of the year.

The deduction for consumer interest is no longer allowed, including interest paid on credit cards and student and car loans.

If you moved last year, you can deduct moving expenses. Full-time workers can deduct most of their expenses if the move is job related. Your new job must be at least thirty-five miles farther from your previous home than your former business location.

You must also have worked at least thirty-nine weeks during the year following the move. If you meet these tests, you may deduct house-hunting costs, including hotels and meals, and expenses related to selling your old house and buying a new one.

And last, if you are claiming a dependent who is five years or older, the dependent must have a Social Security number, and it must be included on your return.

MORE LAST-MINUTE FILING TIPS

You need to examine several areas to avoid making common errors when completing your tax return. They include checking your math and making sure that you've written the correct Social Security number on your return. Also double-check the number of dependents you've claimed. Often, people leave off dependents who may not live with them, such as parents or a child attending school away from home.

Be sure that your W-2s and your 1099s are correct. If they are wrong, have them corrected as soon as possible so that IRS records agree with the amounts you show on your return. Finding mistakes now will save you money and time.

If you have more than one employer, be sure to claim a credit for any overpaid Social Security taxes withheld from your wages. Recheck that you have used the right tax rate table for your filing status.

One simple procedure that can prevent mistakes is to review your return after you have received it from your tax preparer. Next, set it aside for a while, perhaps until the next day. Then, review it again as if you are looking at it for the first time. Not only will this approach help you spot common math mistakes, but you can catch deductions you may have overlooked.

Even though you may have had your return done professionally, this review process is advisable. Everyone, even a CPA, can make mistakes. If you do spot an error, call your tax preparer or the IRS and find out if you can still file the return and amend it later.

ARE YOU LENDING MONEY TO UNCLE SAM INTEREST-FREE?

Did you brag to your friend about the size of your last tax refund? If it was more than $500, you have nothing to be proud of. You loaned that money to Uncle Sam interest-free. That is money you could have used to pay off a debt or deposited in the bank to earn interest.

On the other hand, you don't want to owe the government too much money. If your tax payments do not total at least 90 percent of the tax shown on your return or equal 100 percent of the tax paid the previous year, you could be penalized by the IRS.

If your tax withholding will not be at least 90 percent of your tax bill, you should claim fewer withholding allowances. Increase the number of allowances you claim if the amount of tax due this year will be more than 100 percent of last year's tax.

401(K) CONTRIBUTIONS AND YOUR TAXES

The most tax-favored retirement plan for employees is the 401(k) plan. The reason is twofold.

First, your contributions are before taxes. For example, if your salary is $20,000 per year, and you contribute $1,000 to your 401(k) plan, you will pay taxes on the remaining $19,000.

Second, your earnings in the 401(k) plan grow on a tax-deferred basis. You pay no taxes on the earnings until you withdraw the money.

As an extra bonus, your company may match your contributions. If the company offers a 401(k) plan, make your contribution a priority.

A deductible IRA is the next best choice if you don't have access to a 401(k) plan.

TAX-FREE MUNICIPAL BONDS

If you are concerned about taxes due on interest from your bank accounts or money market funds, consider investing in tax-free municipal bonds. For a taxpayer in the 28 percent bracket, a 7 percent tax-free yield is the equivalent of earning 9.70 percent in a taxable investment.

The 28 percent tax bracket is for married couples filing jointly with an income of $30,000 a year. For single taxpayers, the qualifying income is $18,000.

Many people invest in tax-free municipal bonds by purchasing mutual funds that invest in municipal bonds. The minimum investment in a mutual fund can be as low as $500 compared to a $5,000 minimum to invest in individual municipal bond issues.

TAX TIPS

In 1988, Congress passed the Technical and Miscellaneous Revenue Act. This tax law, nicknamed TAMRA, corrected errors contained in the laws and was expected to raise $4.1 billion in tax revenues over a three-year period. The law affects individuals, businesses, and investments.

For starters, parents who buy Series EE savings bonds to pay for their child's education will avoid tax on the interest the bonds have accrued. These bonds must have been purchased beginning in 1990, and the parents must own the bonds and use them for the child's higher education.

This law also affects older students and their parents. A parent is no longer able to claim an exemption for a student who is twenty-four years of age or older unless that student's income is less than the exemption amount of $2,000. If a parent loses the right to claim the dependency exemption, the student can then claim himself or herself.

TAMRA also devotes quite a bit of attention to business issues. If you are self-employed, you can deduct 25 percent of your health insurance premium but only up to the income earned from the business. That means the business has to be profitable.

None of the cost of the first telephone line you have in your home can be deducted as a business expense, even when you use the phone part of the time for business. However, a second line is deductible when its use is business related. So if you work from your home, be sure you have a phone line solely dedicated to business use.

GET YOUR REFUND IN THREE WEEKS

The IRS has a new system that may allow you to get a refund due you in as little as three weeks. It's called electronic filing, and it eliminates most of the manual processing of traditional paper returns, thereby cutting the time it takes to issue a refund check.

This new system allows qualified tax preparation firms to file tax returns with the IRS over telephone lines. The returns are accepted from these firms directly into IRS computers. Only returns showing a refund can be accepted electronically at this time.

Your refund can be deposited directly into your checking or savings account. The IRS does not charge a fee for this service, but the tax preparation firm may. If you have any questions, call your local IRS office and ask for the electronic filing coordinator.

IS YOUR TAX REFUND OVERDUE?

If it has been at least eight weeks since you mailed your tax return, you can call a special IRS telephone number to find out the status of your refund.

When you call the number, you will need to know the first Social Security number shown on the return, the filing status, and the exact amount of the expected refund.

This service is part of the tele-tax service provided by the IRS and is called the automated refund information service. Call your local IRS office to ask for more information and the phone number for your area.

The IRS also provides free recorded tax information. This service is available by phone and includes information on 140 topics, such as filing requirements, dependents, itemized deductions, tax credits, and other free services.

TAXES AND YOUR MORTGAGE

If you did not qualify for an interest deduction on your home equity loan last year, you may qualify this year. Interest of up to $100,000 of home equity debt is fully deductible. In addition, interest of up to $1 million on a first mortgage can be deducted as long as it is used to buy or improve property. It's all deductible as long as the total debt doesn't exceed the fair market value of the property.

Any late charges you may have paid on a mortgage are deductible. You can also deduct points paid on a loan to make a major improvement in your residence. (A point is a special fee, charged by the lender, which equals 1 percent of the total loan.)

7

PLANNING FOR A COLLEGE EDUCATION

FINANCING A COLLEGE EDUCATION

Pursuing a college degree can be expensive, and finding money for college can prove frustrating and time-consuming. If you know what your options are, the money search could be a lot easier. Odds are that you may qualify for some form of aid, whether it is through grants, scholarships, or loans. First, let's discuss grants.

A grant is like a scholarship. It doesn't have to be paid back. It is based on family need and income. Pell Grants are federally funded and provide a basic foundation for a financial aid package. Undergraduates who attend school at least half-time can receive up to $2,200 a year from a Pell Grant.

Supplemental Educational Opportunity Grants (SEOG) are provided by the college the student attends. These grants don't have to be paid back, but the recipient must attend school at least half-time. Students can receive up to $4,000 per year from an SEOG.

Many students aren't awarded scholarships simply because they don't apply for them. So the most important step in getting scholarship money is doing research to find out where the money is. Once you find the money, you'll realize that you need not be a genius to receive some of it.

Money is available to students with "B" averages, spots in the top third of their high school classes, and above-average scores on one of the college testing programs (900 for the Scholastic Aptitude Test or 18.7 composite on the American College Test). One book students or parents should purchase or browse through at the local library is *The Scholarship Book* by Daniel J. Cassidy. It contains a comprehensive list of scholarship program addresses.

Once you've done the research, my advice is to apply for every scholarship you qualify for. I know of one student who did and received nearly $300,000 in scholarship money.

Loans for College

Here are some loan programs that you should consider. The Stafford Student Loan, formerly the Guaranteed Student Loan, is a government-sponsored program that allows undergraduate students to borrow up to $2,600 for each of their first two years of study. Up to $4,000 is available for the remaining undergraduate years. Graduate students can borrow up to $7,500 a year. The loan does not have to be repaid until the student leaves school or is no longer attending on a full-time basis.

Another popular loan program is for parents of students, the Parent Loans to Undergraduate Students, or PLUS. Parents can borrow up to $4,000 per year with a limit of $20,000 per student.

Home Equity Loans

To finance a college education, you might have to look closer to home. Home equity loans are fast becoming the educational loans of choice. The amount that you can borrow varies with each financial institution. You can generally tap at least 80 percent of the home's value. The advantage of a home equity loan is that the interest you pay is generally deductible on your tax return.

Before embarking on a money hunt for college financing, be sure to contact the student's high-school counseling office for application deadlines and other information. Also, the U.S. Department of Education offers a free brochure that outlines the various types of college aid programs available. Call 1-800-433-3243 to request a copy.

College Work-Study

One of the options offered students as part of a college financial aid package is the opportunity to work their way through school. The college work-study program provides jobs for undergraduate and graduate students who need financial aid. Under the plan, the student will be paid at least the current federal minimum wage. The exact amount will be determined by the type of work and the skills required.

The total college work-study award depends on the total need. The student may work on or off campus, and the employer will usually be a private or public nonprofit organization, or a city, state, or federal agency. The student will be limited in the number of hours he or she can work, depending on the class schedule and academic standing. Contact the college financial aid office for more information.

COLLEGE COSTS

Paying for college may well be the second largest investment a family will make after buying a home. Tuition and room and board at a public college cost an average of $6,000 a year versus $10,000 a year at a private college. The American Counsel on Education reports that both public and private school costs will continue to increase.

Why have college costs been rising? For the most part, the increases are the result of colleges having to raise salaries to keep a first-rate faculty. To meet these rising college costs, some families are borrowing to finance their children's educational needs.

If you have young ones who will not be attending college for five to ten years, a systematic savings plan will help you meet college expenses.

A COLLEGE SAVINGS PLAN THAT WORKS

A recent study by the National Institute of Independent Colleges and Universities revealed that only half the families whose children expect to go to college are saving in preparation for that expense.

The best way to finance an education is to save for it in advance. If you save just $20 a week and earn 7 percent a year for eighteen years, you'll wind up with almost $38,000.

The best way to save is to set aside a regular amount each week or month and treat it as though it were just another bill that comes off the top of your paycheck.

A good idea would be to use payroll deduction plans at

work or to have your bank deduct the same amount each month from your checking account and automatically deposit it in your savings account.

If you don't want to saddle yourself and your children with a mountain of debt, you should start a regular college savings plan now.

A DIFFERENT KIND OF COLLEGE LOAN

Finding money to pay for college is not an easy task today. However, if you are not eligible for federal financial aid or just need additional funds to pay educational costs, you have an alternative. EXCEL and SHARE are two educational loan programs that you should consider. Eligibility is not based on income, but you must have a good credit history and be able to meet current loan obligations.

The applicant can be a parent, spouse, or other responsible person. Loan amounts vary from $2,000 to $20,000 a year with a maximum of $80,000 per student over a four- to five-year period. EXCEL loans can be used at any accredited degree-granting college or university in the United States. On the other hand, SHARE loans may be used only at certain selected colleges.

Loans for Graduate Students

If you are a graduate student seeking money to fund your studies, some loan programs can help you. GRADEXCEL and GRADSHARE are educational loan programs designed to meet the unique needs of students enrolled in graduate and professional degree programs.

A good credit history is a primary consideration, but students with no credit history are also eligible. Loans are based on future projected earnings rather than your current financial situation. In some cases, you can even defer payment on the loan until six months after you graduate.

Loan amounts range from $2,000 to $20,000 per year with up to $90,000 over the length of your degree program. Repayment of the loan can stretch over twenty years, depending on the amount you borrowed.

GRADSHARE loans can be used only at certain selected colleges, whereas GRADEXCEL loans are available for anyone attending any accredited degree-granting college or university in the United States. For additional information, contact the college of your choice.

ACADEMIC TAX TRAPS

Scholarship money may not be free; the IRS may want its cut. Students who are fortunate enough to be scholarship winners may get hit with an unexpected tax bill.

Scholarships are tax-free only to the extent they are used to cover tuition, fees, books, course materials, and other items directly connected with education.

Amounts covering room, board, and personal expenses are taxable. This new limitation applies to scholarships granted after August 16, 1986.

To avoid this academic tax trap, students should keep records and receipts supporting all amounts spent on the items directly connected to education. If challenged by the IRS, students must prove how much of the scholarship money was spent on school items and how much went to cover personal expenses.

EDUCATION AND TAXES

The Tax Reform Act of 1986 reduced the advantage of putting savings in a child's name. Since tax reform, income from investments that exceed $1,000 for children under age fourteen is taxed at the parents' rate. Once a child reaches fourteen, however, the investment income is taxed at the lower child's rate.

But shifting assets to your children may not be a wise move. The College Scholarship Service in New York uses a formula to calculate eligibility for financial help. The formula considers 12 percent or less of the parents' assets to be available to pay college costs but includes 35 percent of the assets listed in the child's name. So, shifting assets to a child may minimize potential future financial aid by making the student's need seem small.

ALTERNATIVE WAYS TO FINANCE A COLLEGE EDUCATION

There are a number of ways to pay for a college education. The interest on home equity loans used for educational purposes is one of the few interest deductions remaining. But carrying the entire burden of funding a child's college education may not be a workable solution.

Here are four alternatives:

1. A sharing arrangement. Expect your children to work part-time while in college.

2. Scholarships and grant programs. Many colleges and universities offer students financial aid.

3. Federal grants, such as the Pell Grants and Supplemental Educational Opportunity Grants.

4. Federal loans, including National Direct Loans, Stafford Student Loans, and Parent Loans to Undergraduate Students.

8

TRAVEL

AIR TRAVEL

What can you do about increasing airfares? Not much! With the deregulation of the airline industry, one would think that increased competition would force airline ticket prices down. Think again! Airfares will continue to rise.

Usually, ticket prices decline after the summer. But this year you can expect to pay more for most round-trip airfares.

In effect, there are now only a handful of major airlines in the United States, and they control the computers that sell the tickets. They have the hubs, the gates at the airports, and the take-off slots. They control the whole ball game.

These airlines offer discount fares only when they compete on the same route with one another. Restrictions on these discounted tickets are becoming greater, so you can look for airfares to continue to increase until airlines get a fair return on their investment or until the industry is more regulated.

AIR TRAVEL AND COMPUTERS

Beat air travel computer bias and get the best airfare or travel package. Travel agency computers show the agent what's available for sale to customers. But agency computers are not independent services. They are owned and operated by large airlines. American and United airlines have their own systems. Other airlines pay the host airline to be listed on the system.

Airlines accuse one another of "computer bias," that is, running information that favors the host airline. The aim is to show the host airline as the cheapest and most available. Sometimes the information is inaccurate, and there isn't much the agent can do about correcting it.

When you deal with a travel agent, find out which airline owns the system the agency uses. Then if you notice the best fares quoted continue to favor that airline, check other sources such as newspapers and other travel agencies that use different systems.

HOW TO GET THE CHEAPEST AIRFARE

Deregulation has forced the airline industry to be more concerned about its bottom line. Making a profit on each flight is necessary. Still, on any given flight, not everyone pays the same price.

We know that the passengers in the first class pay more just to get wider seats, complimentary cocktails, and special attention. But even when flying coach, you will find some passengers whose fares differ by hundreds of dollars. To avoid paying too much for the same flight, you need to know how the game is played.

Airlines use a process called yield management, which starts with a computer program that projects the right combination of fares it will take to fill a flight. The goal is to yield the most revenue from each flight.

Shopping Around for the Best Deal

Shopping for the lowest airfare can save hundreds of dollars, but it will require some time and effort. Here are some tips that can help. Shop early. Start calling the airlines at least a month before you plan to leave. Watch for newspaper ads. Airlines often advertise clearance sales to sell tickets during slow times of the year.

You may get a lower fare by beginning and ending your trip on certain days of the week. Call every airline that flies to your destination and ask for a price. Tell the agent you want the cheapest fare.

After you get one quote, ask if there is a way to get an even lower fare. You may have to leave or return on a specific day. Remember to note any restrictions.

Using a Travel Agent

If your trip involves several components, such as hotel reservations, a rental car, and a sight-seeing tour, a travel agent can help. Consult an experienced travel agent for packaged deals; state exactly what you want to include.

An agent can, by computer, pull up airfares for all the major airlines. Agents earn a commission, usually about 10 percent, for selling plane tickets, hotel rooms, and tour packages. Don't expect a travel agent to spend hours finding the cheapest airline ticket, which will, of course, have the smallest commission.

An especially wise move is to consult a travel agent when going to a city or country with which you are not familiar. The agent can alert you to places to shop and to eat. The agent can clue you in on the places you shouldn't miss and ones you should avoid. Planning ahead and being patient can save you a lot of money on your next trip.

TRAVEL TIPS

Traveling on a budget doesn't mean missing out on the fun. You've probably already made plans for your next vacation, but you may have overlooked some ways to save money.

First, plan ahead as much as possible to take advantage of advance ticketing discounts on airlines. Second, ask your travel agent about budget vacation packages. Third, consider traveling to locations where relatives live and staying with them. You will cut your hotel costs.

When traveling, many people feel that they have to eat at fancy restaurants for every meal. One way to cut meal costs is to eat lunch and breakfast at fast-food places and save the dinner meal for a fancy restaurant. Another alternative is to make lunch your main meal of the day and take advantage of lower lunch prices.

Nationwide, a family of four can expect to pay $180 per day for travel, food, and lodging.

MORE TRAVEL TIPS

If you're going to be doing some traveling, you'll need a place to stay. If relatives haven't extended open arms, hotels are usually your next choice.

Some of today's hotels look more like resorts than places to get a good night's sleep. You'll find pools, nightclubs, exercise spas, and gift shops. These extras make a stay in some of these places as expensive as $200 a night.

You don't need to pay for these amenities if all you want is a clean, safe place to sleep. Several major hotel chains that run luxury hotels also own lower-priced establishments that may fit your budget better. Many budget hotels have all you may need at a price as low as $30 a night. They include Hampton Inn, Motel 6, and Comfort Inn, just to name a few.

AND EVEN MORE TRAVEL TIPS

Presently, there are more than 12 million people who are members of frequent flyer programs. According to a recent study, 75 percent of the frequent flyer bonus awards go unredeemed. Here is a tip on how you can pick up more bonuses.

Refer anyone you know who flies. You'll get extra bonus miles. Carry all ticket jackets from past flights with you when you travel. One of them could very well qualify you for a discount on your next car rental or hotel room.

Just when you think it is safe to use your frequent flyer bonus miles, look out. The IRS is trying to figure out a way to tax you on the value of the free personal travel you take as a result of your frequent flyer miles. So far, the IRS hasn't figured out how to do it. The agency is having problems establishing a set of fair rules for determining the worth of such trips and how to report the dollars.

VACATION PACKAGE TOURS

A vacation package tour contains a number of travel arrangements bundled together. How can you be sure a package tour is a good value?

The key is to find out as much as you can about the tour operator. This behind-the-scenes person puts together the components of the trip, including airfare, hotel, rental car, and sight-seeing, and sells it through travel agents.

Don't be shy about asking questions. The answers could make the difference between a dream vacation and a nightmare. Ask your travel agent if he or she has used this operator before. Was the operator's performance satisfactory?

Carefully read the brochure on the vacation package. Does it feature recognizable hotels or obscure places you have never heard of? Ask friends what packages they have used in the past and if they were satisfied with the arrangements.

EXTRA BAGGAGE PROTECTION

Airlines are notorious for their low level of compensation for lost or stolen luggage. However, there is a way to minimize the possibility of lost luggage before you even get on a plane. It's called excess valuation. But you have to ask for it!

Excess valuation is additional insurance you buy at the check-in counter. It works like this: you set a specific value for your luggage, from $100 to $25,000 per piece, depending on the airline's top limit. The airline will charge a fee ranging from 50¢ to $1 per $100 on the declared value. If the bags are lost or stolen, you'll be compensated at the full declared value. The best feature about using excess valuation is that your bags will receive special attention. Baggage handlers often hand them over personally at your destination, so you can officially sign for them.

HOW TO GET A FREE AIRLINE TICKET

Many airlines offer a free ticket to a traveler who volunteers to get "bumped" or give up a seat on an overbooked flight. The airline will then put the passenger on the next available flight with the original ticket. The free or "bump" ticket can be used for another trip at a later time.

Each airline has different restrictions and guidelines for its bump tickets, but all bump tickets share these characteristics—they're valid for one year after issue and don't require a minimum advance reservation or a Saturday night stay.

Bump tickets have few restrictions, which makes them more valuable than coach or economy fares. Bump tickets can be worth as much as $500 or more if they are used for a long trip. If you are interested in obtaining bump tickets, you should fly with airlines that allow their customers to volunteer to give up their seats at the departure gate.

ANOTHER TRAVEL TIP

You've been piling up frequent flyer miles and anxiously waiting to get your award, a round-trip ticket to anywhere in the country. Then all of a sudden the airline goes belly up! What can you do?

The Frequent Flyer Club offers a program called Award-Guard. It protects frequent flyer mileage and awards only for airlines that fail. Other carriers will honor what you've earned. Call 1-800-487-8893 for more information.

VACATION RENTALS

The next time you're planning a week-long vacation, consider a vacation rental instead of a hotel or resort. You could save a lot of money. Compared to hotels, vacation rentals typically provide more living space and fewer services.

A vacation rental can be an apartment, a cottage, or a villa, and it is often cheaper than a hotel room of comparable size. Rates are especially attractive for families or groups. Two or three couples can easily rent an apartment or a cottage for a week at the cost of one or two days in a hotel.

Renting does not appeal to everyone. Many travelers enjoy the pampering services they receive at a hotel or resort. Some rentals include maid and other guest services as standard features or extra-cost options. Often, you can choose and pay only for the services you want.

Where Are Vacation Rentals Located?

You can find vacation rentals almost anywhere. The majority are available in places like Florida, New York, Hawaii, California, Mexico, the Bahamas, Bermuda, the U.S. Virgin Islands, and parts of Europe.

Three basic kinds of organizations handle vacation rentals—travel agencies, travel clubs, and tour operators. *Travel agencies* are paid by the property owner through a combination of listing fees and commissions. *Travel clubs,* on the other hand, charge annual dues and offer their members additional travel services. *Tour operators* often supply vacation rentals as part of their package tours.

All three organizations provide brochures. Arranging a vacation rental can be as easy as making a hotel room reservation.

Making a Deal on a Rental

When making a deal for a vacation rental, you will have to allow extra time. Often, you'll be asked to arrange a rental up to six months in advance, especially during the peak vacation season. In addition, many vacation rentals require you to stay a minimum of one week. You may have to pay the full rental in advance.

Pricing is usually seasonal, and you can expect to pay less

for longer stays and larger groups. Don't hesitate to negotiate since most rental units don't have a "list" price.

To find the best vacation rentals, ask family and friends for recommendations. They may recommend a specific rental or a reliable broker or agent who helped them out. Another option is to rent through a travel club, travel agency, or tour operator.

9

YOUR BUSINESS

DO YOU HAVE WHAT IT TAKES TO BE AN ENTREPRENEUR?

If you're thinking about going into business for yourself, you must consider many things. First, you have to know if you have what it takes.

All entrepreneurs have one thing in common. They are risk takers. They are people who are willing to put their money, time, and reputations where their mouths are.

To find out if you have the right stuff to be in business, ask yourself these questions:

- Do I have enough self-confidence?

  As an entrepreneur, you must believe in yourself.

- Do I have confidence in my ideas?

  You can't sell anything you would not buy.

- Am I willing to make sacrifices?
  No pain, no gain.
- Do I recognize opportunity?
  How can this work for you?
- Am I decisive?
  You have to be; you're on your own.
- Am I willing to lead by example?
  Don't expect your employees to do anything you're not willing to do yourself.

Now, once you've determined that you have a risk-taking spirit, think about minimizing the risk by holding on to your full-time job. By keeping your job, you can reduce the pressures that face most new entrepreneurs who try to jump into business with both feet. But you'll need a job that gives you ample free time to begin a business.

When considering what kind of business to start, ask yourself about your hobbies that you can turn into money-making projects. What kind of business can you work from home?

Keep in mind that employers don't look kindly on moonlighting workers who might set up a business in direct competition with theirs. So, you may be restricted in the type of business you can start to avoid conflicts with your full-time job. Some possibilities that can work well with full-time jobs include providing child care, taking photographs, landscaping, preparing tax returns, tutoring, and catering.

Sole Proprietorship

There are major benefits to starting your business as a sole proprietorship, that is, a business owned by one person. This legal structure is the easiest and fastest way to get established.

The major advantages include having low start-up expenses, maintaining complete control of the company, and keeping all profits. With a sole proprietorship, you can also stay relatively free from government regulations, and you will face fewer obstacles when selling or going out of business.

But there are some disadvantages. First, personal assets, including your home and car, are liable to creditors. Second, you are completely responsible for contributing all resources and experience. And finally, you may have a harder time obtaining loans if you are the only person lenders can look to for repayment.

Partnerships

A *partnership* is defined as "an association of two or more persons who carry on as co-owners of a business for profit." Partners can be of great help in many areas, adding business experience and assisting in making decisions and obtaining capital.

A partnership is much easier to create than a corporation, calling for much less paperwork to meet government regulations. The disadvantages of a partnership lie in creating the organizational structure, deciding who will hold what position and perform what duties, for example. Also, a partnership puts personal assets at risk.

You should use an attorney to draw up a partnership agreement. How it is written can be crucial later on if one partner attempts to buy out the other or to leave the partnership.

Incorporation

Forming a corporation is no easy proposition. You'll need the assistance of an attorney to set one up.

The major advantages are that with incorporation, it is

much easier to raise capital through loans and the issuance of stocks and bonds. Personal liability will be limited to the amount of your investment. You need to know that the corporation is perpetual, living on beyond its founder's illness or death. Other advantages include the availability of corporate benefits, such as pensions, company cars, and health and life insurance.

On the downside, corporations involve more paperwork, requiring an additional investment in time and sometimes money. Even as the head of the corporation, you have less personal control because you have to answer to stockholders and a board of directors.

OWNING A BUSINESS

Most people, at one time or another, have considered going into business for themselves. The rewards are obvious—job security, a potential for higher income, and pride in ownership. But not everyone is cut out to be self-employed.

Studies have shown that successful entrepreneurs have these characteristics. They are persistent and have good health. They are creative and deductive thinkers. They possess people skills. They have good verbal and writing skills and have the technical knowledge that enables them to build or produce the goods or services needed for the business.

Even these talents and abilities do not assure your success in starting a business. But if you have them, you are ahead of the game.

Selecting the Right Business

For some people, choosing the right business is no problem. Others are constantly seeking ideas from friends and counselors. If you can't decide what business to go into, summarize your background and experience. Then write down what you would like to accomplish in business.

A way to succeed in your own business is to discover something you like to do, learn to do it well, and then find people who are willing to pay for your product or service. In other words, pick the field you know best.

Spend a great deal of time learning the business you want to get into by reading trade journals and making contacts. Also, make sure the business you want to start is in an industry that is expanding.

How Much Money Will You Need?

To determine the amount of money you need to start your business, you must first estimate how much of your product or service you need to sell. Talk with wholesalers, trade association representatives, your banker, and other businesspeople. You should then estimate how much profit you need to earn to make the venture worthwhile. In reaching your final sales and profit projections, don't be too enthusiastic.

Be realistic when estimating sales. Your sales volume will dictate what your expenses must be to handle the projected sales. You don't want to commit to heavier expenses than your sales volume will justify.

To estimate your annual expenses, you need to determine your monthly expenses. Depending on how long it will take to be profitable, you may want to start out with enough cash equal to at least six months' expenses.

Keep in mind that a new business grows slowly, so make sure you have enough cash in the beginning to get up and running. To do this, you will want to prepare a cash-flow statement.

Small businesses run on cash-flow, not profit-and-loss, statements. There are documented cases of businesses that were making a profit but had to shut down because they didn't have enough cash coming in to operate.

The Business Plan

Before you start out in a business, you should have a complete, well-thought-out business plan. A clear, concise plan will help you get the financing you need for your company. It will "sell" the bank on your product or service.

The plan will also act as a measuring stick to determine how well you are doing as the years go by. Your plan should include an overview of your product or service. The marketing plan offers a detailed description of your product concept. The financial outline provides reasonable projections of sales, expenses, and profits.

Seek professional guidance in writing your business plan. Hire an accountant and a lawyer who can lend their expertise in preparing the plan. Later, they can assist you in implementing it.

AFTERWORD

The information presented in these chapters is an offering of help and hope for your personal financial planning and for your life. I believe we can all attain our dreams through self-determination and education. I challenge and encourage you to take what you find useful in this book and put it to work.

Money is merely an instrument, a tool for shaping your life. Getting a grip on your finances takes work and time, but you *can* do it.

I welcome any comments or questions about what you have read here and invite you to share your successes with me at the address below.

For information on additional publications, tapes, or seminars, write to:

Financial Media Services Inc.
70 Fairlie Street, Suite 350
Atlanta, Georgia 30303
404-524-3830